PINK MOON

A Story about Nick Drake

GORM HENRIK RASMUSSEN

TRANSLATED BY BENT SØRENSEN

Robert Kirby *in memoriam*

First published in the United Kingdom in 2012 by Rocket 88,
an imprint of Essential Works Limited
29 Clerkenwell Green, London ECIR ODU

STATENS
KUNSTRÅD
DANISH ARTS COUNCIL

Supported by the Danish Arts Council

Nick Drake's lyrics are reproduced by kind permission of
Warlock Music/BMG Rights Limited

Thanks to Gillie Cunningham for interviewing
Paul Wheeler for the first edition of *Pink Moon*

ISBN (Hardback): 978-1-906615-28-4
ISBN (Paperback): 978-1-906615-29-1
ISBN (ePub): 978-1-906615-24-6
ISBN (Kindle): 978-1-906615-23-9

rocket88books.com

Contents

Foreword

In 1986 I published a biography of Nick Drake in Danish: *Pink Moon – sangeren og guitaristen Nick Drake*. The manuscript of that book was written in 1980–81 and was based largely on interviews I had made with Nick's parents, Rodney and Molly Drake, in their home in Tanworth-in-Arden, Warwickshire, England. It then took me five years to find a publisher who was brave enough to take on a book about a singer, highly regarded by a narrow circle of folk enthusiasts, but largely unknown to the wide record-buying public.

Pink Moon received some good reviews in Danish newspapers and music magazines, but for various reasons the book was never translated into English. I had actually accepted these circumstances and admittedly not given much thought to Nick Drake for twenty odd years when, one day in March 2007, I was approached by Bent Sørensen, associate professor of English at Aalborg University. He offered to translate my book as a *'con amore'* project, claiming that my 80-page text was one of the most precise accounts of Nick Drake that he had read. After a few days of deliberation I decided to embark upon the project.

The book, of course, had to be rewritten. In the meantime Nick Drake had become a huge international star. From the mid-1990s, sales of his records have steadily increased. Songs from his three official albums have appeared in popular TV shows such as *Six Feet Under*, the

BBC has produced radio programmes about him, biographies have appeared, and films have been made about his life and times. The number of Nick Drake websites has become overwhelming.

In my rewriting of *Pink Moon* I have tried to engage with some of the multitudinous facts and opinions that have arisen, concerning Nick's life and his songs, but, dear reader, before you proceed – be warned: this is not a new biography. The pages that follow are my personal story of a songwriter who became something of an obsession to me in my youth; a passion and an artistic mentor all at once.

I have gone through the interviews I made with Rodney and Molly, reread our correspondence spanning eight years, dug out old notes, tapes and articles – in brief, I have cleaned out the attics of my memory. In addition, I have conducted fresh research with Nick's friends and collaborators and made a number of trips to the song-writer's haunts in Marlborough, Cambridge and London, where his life unfolded and unraveled until, at the age of twenty-three, he returned to his parents' house.

I owe thanks to a lot of people for helping and guiding me.

I hope they will all find me worthy of the trust they have put in me.

Gorm Henrik Rasmussen
Copenhagen, April 23, 2009

The original tall, dark and handsome stranger.

**SONGWRITER PAUL WHEELER
ON HIS FRIEND NICK DRAKE**

*But viewed altogether, the artist's works resume their
natural grouping. From death, for instance, they derive their
definitive significance. They receive their most obvious light
from the very life of the artist. At the moment of death, the
succession of his works is but a collection of failures. But
if those failures all have the same resonance, the creator
has managed to repeat the image of his own condition, to
make the air echo with the sterile secrets he possesses.*

ALBERT CAMUS, IN *THE MYTH OF SISYPHUS*

1

*Nick had the most marvellous figure. He was tall, very
tall, about six foot three. His shoulders were broad and
his hips extremely narrow. He had an elegant, very
masculine figure. But he always hunched up his shoulders
and walked with a stoop. And he always wore clothes
that were too small for him. He hated being broad
and he hated being tall. Goodness knows why.*

MOLLY DRAKE

Zeeland, 1978

Whosoever looks for the meaning of it all
must long since have realised
that the meaning of this rustle is this rustle
which in itself is something quite different from
wet rubber boots through leaves...

GUNNAR EKELÖF

On a chilly and rainy autumn night I find myself a visitor in an old cottage in a Zeeland village where a friend
of mine is staying temporarily. We've been for a long walk,
and now we're settling in with a cup of tea, occasionally
scratching our heads, disturbing our pageboy hairstyles
which are not remnants from the Viking age, but rather
token reminders of the youth revolution which unfortunately took place four or five Dylan records too soon for
us to have really been a part of it. From one corner of the
room, quiet acoustic music fills the air. And from our pipes,
waves of scented smoke mingle in the dim light of a single
lamp hanging from the ceiling.

We're discussing a couple of folk musicians that we
both used to follow in our teenage years, Bert Jansch and
John Renbourn. Our habitual argument over which of
the two plays better guitar – the improvisational, bluesy
Jansch, or the classically trained Renbourn – continues

"But how about *this* guy?" my friend asks after a lull
in the conversation, pushing an album cover across the

table. I lean forward and stare at a painting of a full moon. Various objects come floating out of the moon. A teacup, a postage stamp and a clown mask. It looks like a copy of a work by Magritte, the Belgian surrealist painter, or something off a wall from the time when Flower Power was at its peak and the Beatles were on LSD.

No, I've never heard this record, never before have I seen the name printed in small letters across the round moon.

"It's a pink, pink, pink, pink, pink moon" is the sound that comes from a corner of the room. I suddenly realise that this is the record we've been listening to all evening. The sad voice in the background belongs to a guitar player named Nick Drake. My friend tells me that he found the album in a certain record shop that specialises in bootlegs and original pressings of albums from the back catalogues of rock. There, on the floor in the middle of the shop, were stacks of copies of *Pink Moon*.

"A bit of a find, don't you think?"

I lean back in my chair and listen. I must say that my friend is on to something. The guitarist's fingerpicking is really special. I don't recall ever having heard anything quite like it: his nails move across the strings in such a fluid and unusual manner that one might think he had twelve fingers and not ten. But I am even more captivated by his voice and the mood of the songs. The music seems to have been created for a room like this, out in the country. It calls out for contemplation and calm. It is as if these brief, quiet songs creep up on you and strike a note in your mind that you have been longing for without even knowing it. When the stylus reaches the end of the groove, I start questioning my friend about Nick Drake. Who is he? Has he made more records?

"No idea. All I can tell you is that he is dead. He killed himself, a few years ago, I think."

⦙⦙⦙

Sometime after midnight a thunderstorm breaks out. I'm upstairs, unable to sleep. There is no rain, but heavy black clouds race across the sky and at short intervals the landscape is lit up by electric blue flashes of light which grow ever brighter and are followed by increasingly ominous thunderclaps; at one point it sounds as if the trees outside are splitting, one after another.

It is cold in my room and not very comfortable, so I climb out of bed, go downstairs and light a fire in the wood stove. I glance around the living room and the first thing I see is a photograph of Nick Drake; of his face, a frontal shot. It is a photographic negative, an inverted snapshot of the young singer-songwriter, used on the inner sleeve of *Pink Moon*, accompanying the lyric sheet. In the semi-darkness of the room the image seems strangely authentic. And strangely shocking. It's as if you are all alone in a room and then suddenly you realise that there is a cat in there. A black cat staring at you with clear, fluorescent eyes. A nightly visitor without a calling card.

His face is pretty, almost boyishly innocent; elongated, with regular features and a high forehead framed by an unruly, Beethoven-like haircut. His lips, with their finely arched lines, are slightly parted. And again, this mysterious, piercing gaze. What is he trying to tell me? I am over by the window. Outside, the thunder has stopped. The clouds have turned a pale grey, and cover the naked fields like a mottled blanket. None of the stars in the

November sky can penetrate the clouds, but high above the house there is an imprint of something round, an almost transparent, light blue circle. It is only there for a moment, and then slips away behind a cloud formation. While a voice whispers from a corner of the room:

"It's a pink, pink, pink, pink, pink moon."

⁞⁞⁞

One of my other friends owns complete collections of *Melody Maker* and *New Musical Express*. I spend an evening in his basement searching through all the editions. Had I been a secret agent or a private eye or in possession of a large magnifying glass, I might have spotted Nick Drake's name in many announcements of upcoming concerts and record releases. But apart from a couple of very brief reviews of his albums, all I come up with is an ad in the two leading English music weeklies from January 1972, a month before the release of *Pink Moon*. The copy is written by Island Records press secretary David Sandison. In the full page ad Sandison writes about his fascination with Drake's music and his rare, abrupt, encounters with the shy artist. The ad is somewhat unusual in that it seems directed as much towards Nick Drake as at the record-buying audience. It is as if the man from the record company fears that *Pink Moon* will be the guitarist's swan song: now David Sandison wants to get the guy's attention before it's too late and reassure him that Island most certainly will back him up, and are ready to release anything he might want to record.

So look see the days
The endless coloured ways
And go play the game that you learnt
From the morning.

The stylus hits the end of the groove as the black disc keeps turning, filling the room with a monotonous hum, like the sound of the sea on a windy day. You stumble out of bed and take *Pink Moon* off the turntable. As you slip the record back in its sleeve, you encounter that inscrutable face once more.

Who is he? Why do his songs move you so deeply? What is it in you that they touch, so that you sometimes become almost happy in the midst of your misery and temporarily come to terms with the idea that you too will disappear like a spark in a fire?

Is it a sense of connection with a troubled mind or simply that it is OK to isolate yourself in order to feel at home among your fellow human beings? Your inability to break through all the barriers that God or the devil has erected so as to get a good laugh at people like yourself. A guitar-player who may have killed himself, a poet who has looned around the streets; a soul from another country.

He is dead now, he is lost and gone, but his music points the way down endless, coloured roads. A slightly dizzy feeling, a vision of light and shadow. The way the sky looks at dawn when the dark scatters and dissolves. The songs mirror this wonderful shift, just as they reflect the other end of the spectrum. The blue hour when the shadows increase.

Rodney and Molly

It's 1979. And November again. Exactly one year after my first encounter with *Pink Moon* I find myself in London, looking for people who can help me in my quest for Nick Drake. My travel money has come from busking in Copenhagen. All through the summer months, into September and October, I have worked the pedestrian streets with my Western guitar, playing old Dylan and Beatles chestnuts for drunken tourists in the late-night hours. Despite the fact that the intoxicated can often be generous, I've just managed to scrape together enough cash for the ticket and a week at a seedy hotel in Soho.

Island Records have provided me with the address of Nick's parents, but not with their phone number, so I get hold of a Warwickshire directory and find an R. Drake, Far Leys, Tanworth-in-Arden. The name 'Far Leys' mystifies me. Is it a street? Or a manor house, perhaps? A long time passes before the ringing phone is answered.

"Yes, hello?"

The tone is aristocratic, the voice is light and sonorous; no doubt it belongs to an elderly, distinguished gentleman.

"Hello, is this Rodney Drake?"

"Yes, it is. Whom am I speaking to?"

I introduce myself as a young Danish poet, and in my best classroom English I try to explain my plans of writing a book about Nick Drake. Would it be possible to get an interview?

A long pause follows.

"I really don't know if we have got anything interesting to tell you."

It's been five years since the young songwriter swallowed a handful of antidepressants, which had dangerous side effects on the heart. Whether Nick wanted to take his own life or not, whether it was a calculated decision on his part or an impulsive act, are some of the questions I hope Rodney and Molly Drake might help shed some light on. I have a hundred other questions and I believe that I have found the right address.

Nick Drake moved back to his parents' house after recording *Pink Moon* in the autumn of 1971. That was where he chose to stay when things really started going wrong for him; in fact he remained there until his death. I tell his father that I am convinced his son is one of the greatest songwriters to come out of England in the sixties, and that it's a bloody shame his music is not better known. I say that it will not be possible for me to return to England in the foreseeable future.

Rodney Drake hesitates and then disappears from the phone for a minute. As far as I can hear he has a muted exchange with a woman. The only sentence I catch is, "It's a poet from Denmark." A minute or two go by. Then he returns.

"All right, we would like to meet you."

"Ask him if he will read some of his poems!" shouts the woman in the background.

"Did you hear what my wife said?"

I reply that I'll be sure to bring my poems, but that unfortunately they are all in Danish.

"Oh, that doesn't matter. Then you can just translate one or two for us. That'll be fine."

A few days later Rodney and Molly Drake pick me up in Birmingham and we drive through the green landscape of Warwickshire, heading for Tanworth-in-Arden, the village where Nick spent his childhood. The sun is shining from a cloudless November sky. The pleasant atmosphere in the car has an edge of natural awkwardness as we sound each other out. Rodney and Molly are an elegant, extremely polite, elderly couple – she is in her early sixties, he is over seventy, but they appear youthful as they sit in their comfortable car, chatting with me about the culture and music that I perceive as part of *my* history. It is unusual to hear people over fifty referring to Fairport Convention, and the London underground scene of 1967, as if it were the most natural thing in the world. They tell me of the time Nick met the Rolling Stones on a trip to Morocco, and to my utter astonishment they have listened to *Revolver*. They know the individual songs. Molly praises the string arrangements, and Rodney singles out "Eleanor Rigby" as one of the high points of The Beatles Songbook.

In the dozen or so articles on Nick Drake that I'd been able to track down in small, refined, music journals such as *ZigZag* and *Déjà Vu*, I've been reading about the singer's conflictual relationship with the music business, his failed concerts, and his lack of desire for self-promotion. I've been thoroughly informed about his shy, introverted nature and awkward relationships with women, his stubbornness and perfectionism, artistic crises and growing depression. In short, I know quite a bit about Nick as a person, but as for his family background I haven't a clue. What little information I've gleaned comes from a box set of records, which Island released in the spring of 1979, *Fruit Tree: The Complete Recorded Works*. In it the American journalist Arthur Lubow provides an excellent introduction to Nick Drake's musical universe. Lubow characterises Nick's parents as "upper middle class, stereotypically British," and reports that for a number of years the family lived in Rangoon,[1] the capital of Burma, where Rodney Drake worked for a British lumber company. They moved back to England in 1952, settling in a "pastoral village idyll near Coventry," and Nick attended a well-known private boarding school.

We roll through the idyllic village with the church on one side and the pub on the other, while eagerly discussing the influence of J. S. Bach on rock music. When Rodney stops the car in front of a large house at the end of a lane, I realise that we have arrived. This is Far Leys, not a street or a manor, but rather a house with many windows. The solid redbrick walls are covered in ivy. Nick's childhood home. And final abode.

Rodney and Molly lead me down a path to the back of the house and give me a tour of the garden. I'm here in a rural village being shown around a picture perfect English garden. Trees and bushes circle a well-tended lawn; here and there flowerbeds break the straight lines and angles created by the mower. Behind the bushes, more garden: a square lawn especially laid out for playing croquet, the English summer sport. Rodney pauses in the middle of the pitch and for a moment gazes wistfully at the redbrick house with its sloping tiled roof, which looms between the mature trees a few hundred feet away.

---

1   Present-day Yangon, in Myanmar.

"Well, I admit that Far Leys *is* a bit of a handful, no doubt about it. Everything has to be kept up and tended to, and we are not as strong as we used to be. But we care about the surroundings and the people here. Good old Tanworth is *quite nice.*"

We take a moment to enjoy the view from the croquet lawn. The garden opens onto a hilly landscape, cut across with creeks; stubble fields, moss-grown stone fences, little copses and meadows as far as the eye can see. I try to imagine what it must have been like to grow up here. Boys need a lot of space to romp about in. If I were a songwriter and my point of origin was this spot, the likelihood would be that words such as "sky", "sun", "rivers", "leaves", "wind" and "grass" would slip into my vocabulary with the same ease as moving one's feet or drawing a breath.

"Nick would often roam around on his own," Rodney tells me of the early years in Tanworth-in-Arden. "One would find him in the garden or in the meadows behind it. Nick always knew how to amuse himself. I wouldn't go so far as to say that he kept himself to himself or had a hard time making friends – on the contrary we had hordes of kids from the neighbourhood who wanted to play with him. But he was a loner by nature. Certainly not what you would call a herd animal."

In contrast to his elder sister, Gabrielle, who loved colours and company, tea parties and family visits, Nick was an introvert. He was an observer who enjoyed watching the world while keeping it at a safe distance.

"Of course, he couldn't really do that," Rodney continues, smiling briefly, and then turning serious again. "I don't know how to explain this... Nick was so sensitive, so easily swayed. He took the grief and worries of others upon himself, and if anyone he knew were in trouble, he would feel terribly sorry for them. He was the one his friends confided in. When we read him fairytales and goodnight stories he preferred they have a happy ending. If a story was scary or sad he would brood over it for days."

"On the other hand we mustn't forget that Nick had a terrific sense of humour," Molly adds. "It was as if from a very early age he could see through the absurdities of adult life – from the way in which people dress to the discrepancies between what people *say* and what they actually *do*. When I think back on his childhood, that is probably what I remember best. All those hours he and I spent together, laughing."

We have come inside the house and are now sitting between bookcases and mahogany cupboards in a spacious living room. The furnishings bear witness to the years that the family spent in the Far East. There is wicker furniture, Oriental jute mats, strange lamps and bric-a-brac, Chinese figurines, and sofas upholstered in floral patterns. There is a comfortable area with a fireplace; on the black piano in a corner facing the garden is a vase with freshly cut roses. The sun streams in through the many windows. The warm colours of the Orient meet a tasteful traditional interior; the styles of two separate worlds brought together in one grand house.

"Nick had a special sense of humour, it's true," Rodney concurs. He is a tall, powerfully built man with an owl-like head. His movements are slow and dignified. He appears to be a rock of calm as he sits there in his brown cardigan and grey, recently ironed, trousers, his hands folded around his knee, leaning back in the comfortable sofa. At his side sits one who at first glance appears to be his complete opposite:

Molly Drake, a vivacious and delightful lady, gesticulating, entertaining. She is being the hostess, and her husband enjoys that. She speaks passionately about music and tells me that she writes songs as well, as her husband nods and smiles. The couple have been married for 42 years. They are respectful and attentive towards one another. They know each other like a well-travelled duo, and when Molly begins a sentence, Rodney will often finish it, and vice versa. They both speak in this old-fashioned English, which rings clear as a bell with open vowels and voiced Ss, a natural musical tone that leads easily into song. Nick Drake sang in this language. He never adopted any alien accent, even though almost all his musical heroes had their roots in black American rhythm & blues.

"How did he do in school?" I ask.

"Fine," says Molly.

"Amazingly well," Rodney chimes in. "Nick had top grades in nearly all subjects. At his first school, Eagle House in Berkshire where he spent five years, he was elected captain of the rugby team. Later, when he went to Marlborough College, he beat the school record in the 100-yard dash – as far as I know his record still stands."

"He was a fast runner, very fast," Molly nods. "He had the perfect height and build. He was a born athlete."

"The funny thing is that he wasn't really interested in sports," Rodney says. "Neither track events nor rugby were important to him. I mean, Nick never cared about who was in the national team or who went to the Olympics and all that. He was just amazingly fast on the track. Another paradox: our boy didn't like being in charge. He just wanted to potter about quietly and mind his own business. Yet he was made head boy of his class. His classmates loved him.

He was also well-liked among his teachers. But in the last report card he had at Eagle House – an exceptionally good report card – his home-room teacher wrote: *'None of us really knows him.'*"

Molly: "When he changed schools at thirteen, he came home overjoyed and said: 'You know what, Mum, the thing I like best about Marlborough is that I shall have no responsibilities there. Now I can finally relax.' And what happened? His new classmates made him head boy. It was no use protesting. They *wanted* him as head boy."

Rodney hesitates a bit: "Early on in his life there was a pattern emerging. He found himself at the centre of his friends' and teachers' attention, and at the same time he felt that he was an outsider. A strangely uncomfortable position to be in. If you listen to his lyrics, you'll see that *that* is the dilemma some of them deal with."

The Music Room

Rodney and Molly both play the piano. They come from families with musical traditions. After only a short time with them I have the distinct impression that Nick grew up in a household where music was much more than a diversion at tea-time; it was quite simply an important part of family life. Molly wrote songs for her children from the time they were in their cradles. She taught Nick the piano when he was five. Later, when he went to Marlborough, he learnt to play the clarinet and the saxophone.

"It didn't matter what instrument you put in his hand," Molly explains. "The violin, the flute or the trumpet – I think he could coax a melody out of any instrument he got hold of, without any practice at all."

A natural. That is how his parents describe their son. Although it has been five years since his death, I can feel how much he is still present at Far Leys. Nick is here, there and everywhere. Molly goes to the piano and strikes a series of chords. She looks at me inquisitively.

"Way to Blue", I say, feeling slightly disoriented.

"That's right! Nick wrote his songs on the guitar, but 'Way to Blue' is actually a piano piece. When Robert Kirby did the arrangements for the piece, he had the idea of replacing the piano with a string quartet. Nick was overjoyed. We were all very pleased."

There is something puzzling me. When Rodney and Molly discuss when and where Nick wrote something, a number of the songs they keep referring to are quite unknown to me. His parents are throwing about quotes from what appears to be a hidden treasure of songs.

Nick Drake recorded three albums. They are displayed on the table in front of us in their new packaging, next to a little pile of clippings from English and American music magazines. The shiny, deep-blue LP box is gleaming in the sun. *Fruit Tree: The Complete Recorded Works* says the writing on the cover. Molly opens the box and shows me the pencil sketches that depict her son at three stages of his life: Nick, young and hopeful, sitting on the grass; Nick as a grown-up with dark rings around his eyes and black clouds gathering above his head; and finally Nick, the depressive, thin, with hollow cheeks, staring straight through you with his vacant eyes. Portraits of the artist at nineteen, twenty, and twenty-four.

But there was a time before these records, a very creative period where Nick lived in the south of France and spewed out songs like he was Robert Zimmerman number two. As far as I can gather, these songs are simpler and more youthful than the ten that Nick selected for his debut album. The titles sound intriguing. "Bird Flew By", "Mayfair", "Blossom Friend" and "My Love Left with the Rain".

"He met a girl in Aix-en-Provence and wrote a song for her," Molly explains. "The girl's name was Joey. He must have been quite in love with her. It is a song about unrequited love."

"Just like 'Princess of the Sand'," Rodney interjects.

"A lovely one," Molly nods.

"One of his best," Rodney agrees.

"And he never recorded it?" I ask.

"No, not on any album. But we have it on a tape together

with the other songs. You can hear them if you like."

"Rodney managed to smuggle the tape out of the music room and hide it in a drawer," Molly says.

"We had to be very careful, or the songs would have been lost," Rodney continues. "Nick was so hard on himself. He would record a number twenty times and then erase it all. Later he would mock his early songs and call them childish and silly. We, however thought they were wonderful. And we still do – even though the sound quality is very bad."

The door to the music room is open. From where I sit in the living room I can see a music stand, a stool and a small shelf where some tape reels are lying about. On the wall there is a frame containing the original cover of *Pink Moon*. The room has been left more or less as it was on the night Nick left it five years ago, after he had been listening to Bach's *Brandenburg Concertos*. The turntable is still there, and Nick's record collection. While Rodney is kneeling in front of the shelf, looking for the tape of Nick's early songs, I quickly glance through Nick's records. The covers are well-worn. Nick Drake must have been an inveterate coffee drinker, for they all have dark stains and cup marks on them. He has been listening to *The Freewheelin' Bob Dylan* and *Rubber Soul*. Here are albums by Bert Jansch, Tim Buckley, Randy Newman, Miles Davis and Tim Hardin. Van Morrison's *Astral Weeks* has also seen some heavy use. A select, very refined, collection of records, although it gives no clues as to how Nick Drake, aged nineteen, could present a song like "River Man" to his friends in Cambridge. Or how, later, he was able to brew chords together into melodies that practically kept him free of imitators.

"Are you ready?" Without waiting for my reply Rodney

starts the tape. First comes the guitar. The basic riff is immediately catchy. It is simple. The fretwork is virtuoso. Then the words. Nick's voice, muted, darker than one is used to:

Deep down in the depth of forgotten dreams
So far away, so long ago it seems...

"One day he showed up with a guitar; he must have been fifteen or sixteen," Rodney tells me as the tape plays on. "Nick's instruments were the clarinet and the saxophone, so naturally we were curious. He shut himself in this room and started to play. We knew some of the tunes. It seemed as if he found it easy to absorb other songwriters' stuff and he quickly finished with them. But his own songs he played over and over. Often he would practise till late at night, sometimes without switching on the lights when it got dark. He would just sit and strum for hours on end. If Molly and I tried to get through to him, he would just stare absentmindedly at us and mumble a monosyllabic reply."

Rodney must have sensed my fascination with these songs that Nick obviously considered unfinished, because when we have finished our tea and I have met the Burmese housekeeper Naw, he returns to the music room. He comes back from there waving the cassette tape in his hand and gives it to me.

"You can keep this."

I thank him, moved and amazed by this gesture, and ask him if he knows when the songs were recorded.

"1967 and '68," he says without hesitation. "Some are from Nick's time in Aix-en-Provence, but most of them are recorded here at Far Leys – under rather primitive conditions as you can probably hear."

On the way to the station we go by the cemetery at the Church of St. Mary Magdalene in Tanworth-in-Arden, and the couple show me Nick's grave. His plain, grey, arched granite stone carries the inscription "Now we rise and we are everywhere". It stands under an oak tree in the middle of the secluded, rural graveyard; in front of the stone is a bouquet of fresh flowers in a small stand. Rodney bends down and with quick movements of his hand brushes away some wet and golden brown leaves that surround the little plot.

"We were looking for a line from one of Nick's songs that wasn't too sad a memory of his much too early death," Rodney says while rubbing some soil off his hands. "We chose 'From the Morning' because that song has hope in it. It says 'nothing disappears.'"

It is pitch black when we get to Wolverhampton and the two of them accompany me into the train station. We say goodbye. As I wave farewell from the compartment window, I have no way of knowing that in less than a year I would once again be sitting at the living room table drinking tea with them, in an atmosphere so warm and hearty that I almost feel a part of the family...

Over the spring and summer of 1980 we corresponded diligently. My plan to write a biography of Nick Drake had begun to take shape, and the first chapters had already been written.

Rodney and Molly followed my work with a keen interest.

What have the sales of *Fruit Tree* been? I asked. No idea, Rodney replied, we have not received the figures from the record company. Have there been any articles about Nick in the music press? No, not to their knowledge. The breakthrough that his parents had hoped for with the re-release of Nick's three albums in the blue box had, objectively speaking, failed to materialise.

2

You couldn't put anything across Nick. You couldn't cheat him in any way. He would know quickly what you were really thinking. He had a very shrewd way of summing people up.

MOLLY DRAKE

The Guitar

If I were to make a film about Nick Drake I would fill it up with images of lawns and blue skies. There would be cricket games going on for much of the film, and the camera would capture a bunch of young fellows going to the pub, smoking cigarettes, talking loudly, getting drunk and generally acting as if they had found the Philosopher's Stone. A good time would be had by all. Loads of sunshine. Long, lazy summer days by the river.

JEREMY MASON

Nicholas Rodney Drake is enrolled at Marlborough College in January 1962, following a family tradition. His father, grandfather, and great-grandfather had all attended this famous school, which has prepared boys from affluent homes for the best universities in the country ever since it was founded in the middle of the nineteenth century. Politicians, clergymen, military men, civil servants, and poets – great minds and small minds alike have spent part of their youth in this small town in the middle of Wiltshire.

The Marlborough skyline is one of treetops and slate roofs. The landmarks are the grey steeples of St. Mary's Church and St. Peter's Church at either end of the main street, towering like castles in a scene from the days of King Arthur. If one continues west, beyond St. Peter's Church, one reaches the school gates. This is where the town ends and the fields begin. The school is part of the town, yet separate from it. An enclosure of long, red-brick buildings close in on a quadrangle and make Marlborough College resemble a beautiful, old, military establishment with a parade ground in the middle. No doubt, strict rules have been the order of the day here for most of the school's existence, and boys have been disciplined like junior soldiers. The army was waiting for these young men at the other end. And two wars that were to reduce Europe to ruins.

There are dozens of rules in English public schools: house rules, ranks and hierarchies, *fagging* – the latter being among the more spectacular of them, where older students are waited upon hand and foot by newcomers. But, according to two former pupils, fagging was not practised at Marlborough College.

The Empire is crumbling. In the sixties there is, objectively speaking, no longer an Empire. What is left is a class society straining under the weight of a generation of young consumers, the first of its kind in the history of the world. English public schoolboys have started growing their hair long. Their self-confidence is on the rise. At Marlborough, the times are changing with the students.

"A fantastic school," says manager Simon Crocker. "Only one problem. No girls. Girls were a kind of planet we were trying to reach with our spaceships. We only met them in our holidays and at parties."

Crocker, who was a student from 1962 to 1966, met Nick Drake on his first day at school, when they both moved into the same house, Barton Hill, a ten-minute walk from the main building.

"Our Headmaster, John Dancy, later became an important figure within the British educational system. He was a progressive, liberal-minded, visionary who encouraged us to be creative and to believe in ourselves. We were living at the school and had loads of spare time. We put on theatre shows, took drawing lessons, watched films, sang in choirs, and many of us played in various bands. If you were really keen on some activity, the school afforded you a wide range of possibilities."

In such a space, the thirteen-year-old Nick thrives, in the rural setting of Marlborough which so resembles his home. He finds himself among the overgrown hills, much as he did back in Tanworth. On his way from Barton Hill to the main building he sees woods and far-off valleys, he meets cattle placidly chewing their cud on the grassy slopes, and if he turns to face west he sees paths winding their way through green and clay-coloured fields into the horizon; an Eldorado for a lad who likes to roam around on his own.

He develops new interests and makes the acquaintance of Romantic poets such as Wordsworth, Byron, Keats, and Shelley, and perhaps the one most important to him, William Blake, whose rebellious and visionary poetry Molly is later to single out as one of the early sources of inspiration for her son. Nick is polite, courteous, and gentle as a summer breeze. His favourite subject is English. In the classroom, the engineer's son shines in his use of language, and his beautiful, flawless pronunciation. Nick is *particularly* fond of the breaks in the school's weekly schedule. As a boy who is contemplative by nature he has no objections whatsoever to Tuesday, Thursday, and Saturday being half-days, and Sunday – except for church attendance – being kept free. There is plenty of time for games, and young Drake excels on the sports field with his long legs, out-sprinting all his peers.

"Probably one of the best sprinters we have had since the War," his teacher and House Master, Dennis Silk, writes a few years later in his recommendation of Nick for Cambridge University. "And yet he would more often than not be found reading when he should have been training."

But it is not just poetry that tempts Nick away from a glorious career as a sprinter. He has brought his clarinet from home, and at the start of term he has registered for classes with a music teacher specialising in the instrument, a real character by the name of Eddie Douse. Douse will also teach Nick how to play the saxophone and after a while he joins the school's marching band.

"The College Cadet Force was a bit of a joke," says Simon Crocker, and chuckles. He scratches his neat little moustache and cocks his head. He is a tall man, very approachable and energetic, with an easy smile. He is sitting in the offices of Mount Pleasant Studios in London, and as he talks about his schooldays, secretaries scurry in and out of his office and the phones outside beep like a minor electronic symphony. But Simon Crocker is not in any hurry. He takes his time telling these stories from the sixties, when a group of young men were trying to gain a foothold on a restless planet.

"Neither Nick nor I cared for the military. We were essentially pacifists. This whole idea that if war broke out we would all automatically become army officers seemed rather ludicrous to us. We could not take it seriously. That's why we would introduce Motown songs into the repertoire of the marching band; and let's face it, it was quite hilarious to see forty boys in uniform march around to the strains of The Supremes' 'Where Did Our Love Go'. Also, when the whole cadet force was lined up for our annual inspection by some famous General or Air Marshall, we had to stand to attention for a long time and inevitably, as it was in the heat of summer, a number of boys always fainted. So, playing pop hits to the background noise of people dropping their rifles and clattering to the ground was very funny too."

In the spring of 1964, Nick and Simon form The Perfumed Gardeners[2] together with three of their friends. Nick plays the piano and the saxophone, Simon is on drums and harmonica; apart from them there is a bass player, a lead guitarist, and a rhythm guitarist – and they occasionally add a horn section. The band performs at balls and soon becomes a regular feature at the school's monthly film nights. The Gardeners play to a capacity crowd at Memorial Hall who groove to the tones of jazz classic *St. James Infirmary Blues*. The showpiece is an intensely rhythmical version of "Parchman Farm", a song John Mayall and The Blues Breakers will record years later with a bright young guitar talent named Eric Clapton.

"Nick chose the material and did the arrangements," Crocker explains. "He was a far better musician than the rest of us. He knew that, of course, but he never bragged about it. He was the born bandleader. In addition, he was the only one among us who could carry a tune. Nick's voice was never poppy or mannered – it was simply *cool*."

Some weekends the boys go down to London, spending evenings at crowded clubs in Soho where they encounter one of the hottest new names of the time, The Graham Bond Organization. Nick loves the sound of

---

2   After *The Perfumed Garden*, the well-known early 16th-century Arabian text on the art of making love, by Sheikh Nefzaoui.

Bond's Hammond organ. He likes the jazzy way in which the band plays rhythm and blues – Jack Bruce's improvisations on electric bass and Ginger Baker's storm of percussion and counter-rhythms, a partnership soon to take centre stage in the rock band Cream. It's 1965 and LSD is still just a random set of letters to these boys.

Simon Crocker: "The school had an 'official' pop band which performed in uniform suits and did all they could to sound like Gerry and the Pacemakers. That wasn't our cup of tea. We saw ourselves as the Marlborough Rolling Stones. If you listen to the first two or three Stones albums, you'll discover how much Mick Jagger and Keith Richards owe to black music. We were both interested in rhythm & blues, a style of music which was basically off-limits to English radio. Black R&B records were hard to come by, so we were listening to the white versions of this music: Manfred Mann, Georgie Fame, and The Animals. Nick was also a big fan of the pianist Mose Allison. That particular blend of jazz and rhythm and blues fascinated him."

▮▮▮

Back in Marlborough, as he is strolling down the High Street one day, Nick spots a steel-stringed guitar in the window of Salisbury's, the town's big two-storey music shop that sells instruments, sheet music, and gramophones and records. "£13" reads the price tag, tucked between the strings. The tall college boy in his too-short tweed jacket, tight jeans, and pointy, black leather shoes stops and stands there for a moment, staring into the shop.

It's a brand new guitar. It's shining in the afternoon sun. It has feminine curves and a long, dark brown neck, adorned with tiny, round, mother-of-pearl position marks. He is wondering what it would be like to *hold* that guitar, rap his knuckles against the shiny wood, strum the strings, and run his fingers up and down the fret board. He has long considered getting a guitar. He has already learned four or five chords and listened to Bert Jansch and Donovan. The songs on Dylan's latest album *Bringing It All Back Home* have given him a lot to think about. More than that, they have changed his way of understanding the world, without him fully realising how and why. "Mr. Tambourine Man" is a damn fine poem. That much he knows. Chains of mysterious, inscrutable rhymes, four chords, and a tune so simple that it almost hurts.

He gets out his wallet and starts counting the notes and coins.

He has exactly the sum required. A sign from above, or just one of those coincidences that life presents which force a person to make a choice? Or should Nick, the schoolboy, choose to do without? The thing is, his pocket money has to stretch all the way to the autumn break when he returns to Far Leys. He scratches his head, squints. As he approaches the door to Salisbury's he breaks out in a sweat. Ready to give up the smokes? No parties, no concerts, for *two* months? Live like a monk for the foreseeable future? Should he go to Dad and ask for "a small loan"? Is he willing to humiliate himself for an object everyone will be quick to tell him he doesn't need?

The band already has two guitarists. They play rhythm and blues – not folk music. Besides, he has promised Simon to go with him to London this weekend, and who wants to spend a whole evening at the 100 Club with just a glass of tap water?

With a rather crestfallen yet determined look on his face, Nick puts his wallet back in his pocket. By the time he reaches the City Hall at the end of the High Street he spins around. It is as if a magnetic force is pulling him back to Salisbury's. Ten minutes later he exits the store, carrying a long black case in his hand. It is heavier than he had imagined. He is dragging it along, casually, as if he were a seasoned musician on his way to yet another gig. Outside The Royal Oak he bends his knees and lowers the box down gently in the middle of the sidewalk. It's a normal Wednesday afternoon; people are passing by with their briefcases and grocery bags, caught in their own routines. The locals from the town meet in coffee shops and tea rooms up and down this, one of the widest streets in England. A bunch of boys in school uniforms make their noisy way towards River Park. It's getting on for five. Nick picks up his guitar, homeless and at the same time at home; a troubadour with his entire fortune hidden in a black case. He could take out his guitar, stand on the nearest street corner, and wail out his pain or express his sudden joy at being alive.

The songs are already there. They are floating in the air in front of him. All Nick has to do now is learn how to play them.

♪♪♪

"It was Dylan who brought us together," says Jeremy Mason one day in April 2008, some forty years after he, Simon Crocker, and Nick Drake left Marlborough College to go to France and study abroad.

Mason is sitting in his stand at the antiques market in Davies Mews near Oxford Street, like a wizard in his cave.

From floor to ceiling there are showcases with cast-iron Buddha figurines, Chinese porcelain vases, and fragile clay statuettes of gods and dragons. Nick's school friend is now sixty. He is a well-dressed gentleman with a reddish moustache, which is slowly turning grey, and a nose that shows character. His eyes are bright and curious. He is used to canvassing the punters; sniffing out potential customers. "Oriental Art" says a glass plaque in his window facing the mews, where businessmen and Chinese tourists in suits and ties jostle for space.

"We used to take long walks up and down Marlborough High Street, while smoking cigarettes and discussing the lyrics to 'The Times They Are A-Changin'". We saw ourselves as outsiders. We read a lot and took life very seriously – a girl you had kissed at a party, a verse from one of the Liverpool poets, Jean-Paul Sartre, Oscar Wilde's novels, or a letter which arrived with a few words written on pink stationery; all of that seemed tremendously important."

The antiques dealer smiles wryly. He pauses for a second.

"In reality we were a couple of perfectly ordinary blokes among eight hundred teenage boys who all wore more or less the same clothes, had more or less the same haircut, and all came from nice, English, middle class families. One had to come up with something extraordinary to stand out. Nick and I worshipped Bob Dylan. His songs became the platform from which we operated, at least at the beginning of our friendship. We would hitch down to London on weekends, go to concerts in the nightclubs and spend a lot of time in record shops where we would buy albums by John Coltrane, Thelonious Monk, and Sonny Rollins. In the evenings we would listen to *Christopher Logue Reading*

Poetry to Jazz. We thought it was a new record, but it turned out to have been made in the fifties."

▲▮▮

The guitar feels good in his hands. And Nick has time. Half days off, or sometimes whole days, while his mates run around the sports field. And dark autumn nights when the rehearsal rooms below Memorial Hall are empty, because the bands have all gone out for a pint in one of the many pubs in this medieval town. In a few months he develops a technique that will make seasoned guitar players shake their heads in sheer bewilderment if they were to try and imitate his style. Nick has long and nimble fingers, and they dance over the strings in ever-changing rhythmic patterns.

During the holidays he sits in the music room at home and churns out twelve-bar blues, and ballads whose origins are lost somewhere in the Mississippi delta where black farm workers sang out their anger and pain under the open sky. There is something about the blues that hits Nick hard. Perhaps it is the loneliness and the feeling of being completely broken, in this style of music, that invites a man so persuasively to explore with his guitar. Perhaps it is the fact that in the essence of the blues there is a joy at being alive, an often thinly veiled homage to the free, vagabond life.

He unearths the great British treasure trove of songs and finds traditional folk songs and sea shanties, arranges them in new versions and records the whole mix on his Tandberg reel-to-reel. He sings duets with his elder sister Gabrielle, while the two of them make plans to perform together. He tunes his guitar to an open string E minor and sits around long after midnight running his fingers up and down the frets, playing the same riff over and over until his index finger starts to bleed. He learns "Don't Think Twice" and "Tomorrow is a Long Time", and tracks down those exact Woody Guthrie classics and country blues standards that allowed a folk musician named Robert Zimmerman to become Bob Dylan in March 1962.

The tunes are there, but Nick still doesn't have the words.

He is patient enough to wait. And wise enough to know that the best lines are the ones that come when you have stopped trying to force them down on paper.

⁂

"Nick Drake was a good listener and I was a good talker," Jeremy Mason recalls. "Nick would observe the world around him discreetly; I preferred to jump right in. We were chalk and cheese. I think that is why we got along so well."

"And what would we talk about, then, you'll probably want to know? What topic did we always discuss endlessly?" The antiques dealer holds his breath. Then, in sonorous English: "*Girls!* And what did we do about it? Not a thing!"

It wouldn't have been easy for the two schoolmates to start affairs with fifteen- or sixteen-year-old girls. The fact is that the first female students were only allowed inside the walls in 1968. Until this decisive year Marlborough College remained an institution populated by one gender only: Men teaching boys. Full stop.

"I've never been able to work out if that was a good thing or a bad thing," muses Jeremy Mason. "Our society of today would probably judge the school harshly. One would claim that we were oppressed and ruined – whole cohorts of English middle class boys gone queer, forced into homosexuality. But that is not how I saw it at all. A daily routine without females of our own age afforded us a chance to contemplate things. We had peace and quiet to read. We had time to learn how to play an instrument and develop friendships. Personally, I developed a passion for various artists and writers, something I have maintained until this very day. And as for the girls, they weren't going anywhere. They were waiting for us with the same curiosity and eagerness as we were anticipating them."

Nick's favourite subject is still English. He has a hard time conjuring up the necessary discipline in subjects that don't interest him, such as Latin, History, and British Constitution. He writes poetry, goes to art galleries with Jeremy, and for a while is very taken with the paintings of French symbolist Pierre Bonnard. However, Nick's lack of enthusiasm in class in no way means that he has lost the confidence of his classmates. The engineer's son is voted House Captain. Through several terms he gets up at seven every morning and wakes the boys up in Senior House C, the oldest building of the school. In the evenings he is the man who locks up and puts the lights out. He does the rounds of the dormitories, and makes sure that even the biggest troublemakers are in bed. According to the house rules, curfew is at quarter to eleven.

In his recommendation of Nick to Cambridge, in October 1966, House Master Dennis Silk writes: "He was someone who everybody liked enormously here, despite his reticence and the difficulty of getting to know him well." Silk does nothing to hide the fact that through the years he had great expectations of young Drake, and that these were not always fulfilled. Laziness? Lack of bookish interests? The House Master emphasises that during his last year at Marlborough, Nick really pulled himself together. He describes his student as a daydreamer, a boy with musical and artistic talents, and he concludes: "He could give a lot to the community as well as getting a lot. He is a most delightful person to deal with."

⚏

"Nick often said that there would be a revolution in 1980," Rodney says. "He would read books about the rise and fall of the Paris Commune, and I think he was the best student in his class in French. Later he began to be interested in the writings of Charles Baudelaire. He read the poems in the original language. Molly had a Linguaphone French course. Nick would always return to that course when he wanted to freshen up his language skills. He loved France. We all do. It runs in the family."

In his summer vacations Nick goes across the Channel to the Promised Land. He visits Jeremy Mason whose parents own a house in Provence, near the historical town of Pont du Gard. In August 1965 he hitchhikes from Paris to Avignon with a friend from school, and the two of them continue down the Mediterranean coast until their money runs out. The next year he gets his driver's licence. He borrows Molly's car, a Morris Minor, and sets off into rural Provence where the wine is cheap and bars and cafés are shoulder to shoulder in little labyrinthine towns, and where the mountains loom like staircases leading into space.

In the summer of 1966 Nick passes his exams at Marlborough; truth be told, not with very impressive results, but good enough for him to read English at one of the top universities in the world.

The autumn months Nick spends back home in Tanworth-in-Arden and at friends' houses.

Rodney: "As far as I can recall it was Simon Crocker's parents who brought up the topic of Aix-en-Provence. The thing was that Nick was due to start at Cambridge University in September of 1967, and that was almost a whole year away – an awful lot of time for a restless young man to kill. He was in constant opposition to Molly and myself, although you cannot say that he was hostile in any way. Basically Nick was very easy to get along with."

Rodney's gaze grows distant as he sits there staring at the clippings spread out on the table. "In search of Nick Drake", one of them reads. The accompanying photo shows his son, shoulders hunched, his back turned, heading towards a lake.

"But he didn't have the energy to discuss things with us. We represented a part of society he wanted to distance himself from. And the idea of combining a stay in the South of France with language studies sounded exciting to us. The university in Aix-en-Provence had specialised language courses for foreign students. So, one day shortly after Christmas we sent the lad off to London where he was going to meet up with some of his friends from Marlborough College. He brought his guitar along."

Molly: "It was in Aix he began to write songs."

Rodney: "That's right. That's where it started. He came home after six months in France, and it seemed as if his life had turned around completely. He hardly got through the door before he sat down right here in the living room and began playing for us…"

Molly: "'Bird Flew By' was one of those songs, wasn't it?"

Rodney: "Yes – and 'Princess of the Sand' and 'My Love Left With the Rain'."

▮▮▮

Simon Crocker and Jeremy Mason were waiting at Victoria Station on that cold, grey morning of January 1967. They both recall their nervous energy and all the expectations they had of France; going abroad was quite an adventure.

"This was the first time we had really left home, I mean been on our own out in the great big world," Simon remembers. "There was no one to watch us, no worried parents, no teachers or siblings interfering with us. We were as free as birds. It was fantastic. When we got to the other side of the Channel, we discovered that the French actually spoke French, and if you thought you could get by with English you were sadly mistaken. Nick could just manage to have a conversation on an everyday level; the rest of us had to get by with sign language. We soon learned not to advertise where we came from. General de Gaulle had just pulled France out of NATO. That man hated Britain and the USA. In short, as Englishmen we were living a somewhat precarious existence, and one of the first things that happened was that the police stopped us. They asked to see our passports. That was quite unpleasant. We found out that the best strategy was to play dumb. From then on we always pretended that we had forgotten our identity papers. We said that we were Dutch or Swedish. That actually saved us from being dragged down to the police station."

Simon Crocker laughs. These stories of a Europe torn by power struggles and age-old conflicts seem laughable in an era where trains shuttle back and forth between London and Paris, and where it takes an uncommon interest in Customs rules to know where the boundaries between the various EU countries actually run. In 1967 Spain was a Fascist dictatorship. And right down the middle of the continent ran the Iron Curtain, separating East from West, the good from the bad, or vice versa, all according to one's political convictions.

Aix-en-Provence is a town full of fountains. Here are squares, galleries, olive trees, and old picturesque houses. Much water. Many colours. Much light. Paul Cézanne was born in Aix. In these sun-drenched surroundings the Father of Modernism led his own quiet life, painting pictures no one wanted to buy. Cézanne had his studio right across from the city cathedral. On the main street is Les Deux Garçons, the café where the Impressionist painters from Paris would sit and get drunk as they made sketches on their drawing blocks and discussed the affairs of the world. "That soon became our regular café," Crocker recalls.

"After a couple of weeks of barely scraping by, we managed to find a couple of cheap flats in a project called Residence Sextius. The block was behind Place Vendôme, about a ten-minute walk from the centre of town. Each flat had one room, a bath, and a balcony. We turned one of them into a bedroom and the other into a common room, and since we were constantly broke, we had to share everything. Food, books, cash, booze, and records: it all went in a shared pot. We had parties and met new people. There were many English people in town, young, eccentric, upper-class types who were enrolled in university for one reason only: to get cheques sent over from their rich parents, because as a tourist you were only allowed to bring £50 with you out of England."

When asked how the language studies were going, Jeremy Mason frowns briefly. He sits for a few seconds and stares thoughtfully into space. "Hmm, I actually can't remember. I don't recall the university. We *must* have been there at some point, probably right at the beginning. And it was no doubt horribly boring. I bought a sketchbook and started drawing. My very first drawing is of Nick with his guitar, sitting on the bed in our flat."

♪♪♪

He sleeps late, spends the afternoons on the couch with Baudelaire's *Les Fleurs du Mal* in one hand and his guitar in the other. He is writing poems about sunsets and unresolved love affairs, songs whose finely masked net of nostalgia and light melancholia seem to have been created in the subdued atmosphere of late night open air parties.

Sometimes he takes his instrument under his arm and pops down to one of the town squares and plays for the tourists and café patrons; occasionally Jeremy tags along and passes the hat. Nick has begun to play in small clubs in the old part of town, cabarets and folk clubs frequented by lots of foreign students. One night he meets a nineteen-year-old woman from Miami, Florida – a guitarist and songwriter like himself. Her name is Robin Frederick. They play together a few times and she teaches him a blues song, "Been Smokin' too Long", which is about opium and pot use. Whether the lyrics draw on Frederick's own experiences is not clear, but the song is her own work, and it makes a strong enough impression on Nick for him to subsequently record it on his tape machine back in Tanworth-in-Arden.

On warm nights in spring one finds Nick, Jeremy, and Simon in the artists' hangouts in town, in the company of students and would-be poets, young rebels and eccentrics chasing experiences under the sky blue lanterns of the south. One Friday in March Nick is in a café on his own. For once without his guitar. The red wine flows freely, and under the tables there is a lot of fumbling around with cigarette paper and tobacco. This is no ordinary tobacco; where it comes from is an open question. The leaves are a dark green and smell of resin.

From the jukebox comes "Strawberry Fields" – John Lennon's voice veiled, strangely distorted…

Nothing in the room seems real, and there's certainly nothing to get hung about. Across from Nick sits a fellow from California, relaxed, sun-tanned, and wearing a shabby straw hat which he has brought with him all the way from Berkeley Art College. The stranger tells stories from his homeland, talks about a whole new lifestyle which has gained ground over there, in San Francisco to be precise, where men and women run around with flowers in their hair, and where musicians move in with one another in great communes and give themselves strange names such as Jefferson Airplane and The Grateful Dead. Nick, whose head is still ringing with the songs from *Highway 61*, interrupts the American with a remark that not only in San Francisco are things changing; but everywhere.

"But the fruits will not be harvested until later," he explains.

The Berkeley student pushes back his hat and stares at this tall, young man with mussed hair.

"What are you talking about?"

"The revolution."

"Are you a Communist?" The American wants to know.

"Nah."

"What then?"

"Folk singer," Nick replies.

After midnight he roams the streets with a couple he has met through some friends and friends of friends; two posh bachelors who have both gone to Eton College, which includes heads of state and members of the Royal Family among its alumni.

Nick is a little stoned and feeling good. The trio end up at an Arabian nightclub where they bump into a flock of students: English, American, French, ready to party, shoulder to shoulder, each and every one of them apparently on a collision course with Lyndon B. Johnson, General de Gaulle, and all the other powerful men of this world who deal in nuclear arms rather than friendship.

The smell of cigarette smoke is mixed with the spicier aroma of exotic tobacco, and there is a brisk trade in every corner. Money changes hands and is pocketed. Tiny white and pink pills are exchanged. Some of the students remain seated for hours on end, just staring into thin air, while others rush out into the deserted streets as if they were chased by demons or ferocious animals.

The Moon hangs like a blind eye in the sky.

The Moon over Aix-en-Provence sees nothing, except its own mirror image in the city windows; as the shiny ball slowly floats away, its beams fall like a silvery rain, splintered in a thousand fountains.

At sunrise Nick saunters home to the flat behind Place Vendôme. He is too restless to sleep and sits down to write songs in the dawning light. He writes about the girl who betrayed him tonight and who will most likely betray him again tomorrow, the dark and ambiguous Joey: *Who she would run from you never will know...*

One day Jeremy steps into the bedroom and finds his bed upright, blocking the balcony door. On the floor Nick sits cross-legged. A smile plays around the corners of his mouth.

"What's going on?" Jeremy asks.

"Nothing much."

"But why have you barricaded the door?"

"I can fly," Nick replies. "I put your bed there to keep myself from doing it."

A Trip to Africa

Richard's tale

In the spring of '67 I studied at the Institut Botanique in Paris, mainly to learn some French which, however, quickly became a complete wash-out. In addition to that I was constantly broke. I met a lot of Englishmen and got into a small clique of rather strange types, and suddenly one day a guy I had just met pulled up in an old battered Ford Cortina GT. His name was Mike. His full name was Michael Hill, I think – he was a Lord or something like that – an aristocrat, you know, well-bred, but definitely no family fortune.

"Let's go!" he said

"Go," I said, "where?"

"We're going to Chad," he said.

"Where is that?" I wondered.

"In Africa," Mike said, "somewhere south of Morocco. We'll pop down there and see what's happening. We'll be back again in a month."

"Great," I said, "I'm in."

I hurried to pack a suitcase, and we drove out of Paris heading for the south of France. Mike told me that we were picking up a couple of friends of his in Aix-en-Provence, where he himself was a student, or at least had been one – at the university – but don't ask me what he was studying. OK, I thought, the more the merrier; there is enough room in the back seat. We spent a night in Aix-en-Provence, and the next morning our two travel mates joined us. One was a

57

tall, slim, fellow with a guitar; he politely introduced himself as Nick Drake. I liked him immediately. He seemed modest and a bit reserved, yet mysterious; there was something terribly attractive about his ways. The other fellow's name was Bob. That is about all I recall about him. He was English and seventeen years old like the rest of us. We jumped into the car and took turns driving down through Spain. We rattled over the Pyrenees, crawling along at a snail's pace on miserable little mountain roads. I had just got my licence and that rule of theirs of keeping the car on the right-hand side was bloody hard to get used to.

Somehow we made it to Tangier. All four of us were completely broke. My mother was terribly worried. I hadn't told her where I was going, but every time we came to a major town I wrote to her, and the gist of every letter was "Send more money." She did what I asked her. As a loving mother she really didn't want her son to die of starvation in a foreign country. So I had a cheque from her every now and then, and I assured her that we remembered to brush our teeth and do the laundry and all that.

I recall the small, filthy, Arab hotel rooms with cockroaches crawling up and down the walls, those nights we spent in the car, four guys squeezed together in ten square feet, tossing and turning in the seats, trying to get a few hours of sleep, and I remember the Moroccan grass which smelled like camel shit and pretty much tasted the same way, but none of that mattered since we hadn't gone down there because we wanted to get stoned, but because Africa is an adventure.

So, we parked the Cortina in one of the labyrinthine streets of Tangier and the first thing we saw was a crowd of people outside a hotel, and someone yelling: "The Rolling Stones are here!" I took a look around. In the middle of the crowd I spotted Cecil Beaton, the fashion photographer, old, dignified, very British, towering over the rest with his white hat. He was flanked on one side by Paul Bowles, on the other by Anita Pallenberg. When I saw this slim, astonishingly beautiful German-Italian actress, I started thinking: "There must be some truth to this. The Stones are around, because why else would Pallenberg be in Tangier?" She was Brian Jones' girlfriend. Later I heard that this was the trip where she dumped Jones for Keith Richards, although there have also been rumours that she was sleeping with Mick Jagger, too.

I hadn't read Kerouac. My knowledge of the Beat Generation was very limited, and I honestly don't think any of us had any idea that there was a whole colony of American writers in Tangier, and that people like William Burroughs, Allen Ginsberg, and Gregory Corso had been living in a waterfront hotel there, on and off during the fifties and the early sixties. But all four of us had a clear feeling that we were in the right place at the right time. Tangier was oozing magic. Tangier was hip in the same way that Paris was hip at that time, and one felt that *this* was where things were happening. Everyone we met seemed happy and relaxed, and Nick played his guitar while we sat in the sun, smoking joints, flipping out over the camels and minarets and snake-charmers and the Moroccan women swaying by in their long colourful dresses, and all this teeming life was so overwhelming; there we were on the tip of Africa like an outpost of *the summer of love*, hippies without knowing it, young, happy, hungry for experience, the world unrolling before our feet like a magic carpet.

We stayed in Tangier a few days. Then we drove west to Marrakech where we got rooms at a hotel in the Arab quarter. We were pretty beat up after the trip and we went out to find a place to eat. We went into the first restaurant we saw, and there, in one corner of the room, were Cecil Beaton and Anita Pallenberg, along with Brian Jones and Keith Richards. There were several other people around their table, maybe ten or twelve altogether, including a number of beautiful sexy women, and of course we were all fired up. I mean, this was the second time in one week that we bumped into one of the world's most famous rock bands, in Morocco of all places. We felt that the time had come for us to get introduced. But how to create contact? That's where the guitar came in. Nick was always carrying his guitar around, and he rarely let it out of his sight, perhaps because he was afraid that his precious instrument would get stolen.

"Now, you go over there and play for them a bit," Mike said. "Entertain The Rolling Stones a little; show them what you can do."

"Great idea," Bob said.

"No, no, I couldn't," Nick said, with a look of horror on his face.

"Oh yes, you can – come on!"

"It's going to get terribly embarrassing," Nick was mumbling. "Forcing myself upon them, like that … I couldn't possibly…"

He bit his lip in apprehension, glancing over at the table where the Stones and their ladies were toasting with champagne. Then Bob gets up and goes straight over there and announces: "My friend here would like to play a few songs."

We had to almost shove Nick across the restaurant. He sat down at the end of the table, all flushed with embarrassment, played two or three songs, Dylan or Donovan; certainly none of his own songs. People applauded politely, and Keith Richards praised his guitar playing and said: "If you come to London, be sure to look us up," and so on. We had a marvellous evening. And when the waiter brought the bill we were hoping that The Stones would pick it up for us, but unfortunately that didn't happen.

A couple of days later we set off for Chad. We drove south with no clear notion of where that country was exactly. If we had taken the trouble to look at a map of Africa, we would have discovered that we would have to go through Algeria and Niger – actually, more than a thousand miles through the Sahara desert – to get to our end goal. The mood was tip-top, although we carried no water or provisions of any kind. When we got to the Atlas Mountains the Cortina suddenly started wheezing and coughing, and right there, on one of the dusty roads leading to the desert, the car stopped. We got out, and a cursory examination led us to conclude that the engine had broken down. So, we sat by the side of the road and waited. I think we had landed in one of the most deserted areas of Morocco. There were no settlements for miles around, just rocks and goats. The sun was glowing from an impossibly blue sky. Then, from out of nowhere a jeep appeared, and luckily for us the driver was a very helpful and friendly man. He got a rope attached to our bumper and towed us to a town called Meknès where we managed to find a garage. The mechanic was staring at our long hair with an astonished look on his face.

"Are you The Rolling Stones?" he said in broken English.

"Yes," Mike said firmly. "We are The Rolling Stones, that's absolutely right."

Nick pulled out his guitar and began to play, and the mechanic asked if he could take a photograph of us, which of course we made no objections to. He fetched his camera and the four of us posed with him in front of the battered old Ford Cortina. When we came back after about a week and the car was all fixed up and parked outside his garage, the man would not accept any payment from us. The only thing he insisted on was another photo of The Rolling Stones and himself, sitting behind the wheel.

We drove back to Tangier and from there on to Aix-en-Provence, where we dropped Nick and Bob off. Mike and I said our goodbyes in Paris. Although we'd had a smashing trip I never expected to see any of those guys again. I went back to studying French, and around mid-summer I went back to England. I was going to study Medicine in Cambridge and had been admitted to Trinity College. The very first day in my new room – I still hadn't had time to unpack – there was a knock on my door. And in steps Nick.

"I'll be damned," I said, "what are you doing here?"

"Studying," he says.

"In Cambridge?"

"Yes."

"What subject?" I asked.

"English," he replied.

"Excellent," I said, thinking to myself: Come on! We have been on the road together for over a month. We've slept in lousy little hotel rooms, we've been cooped up in that car day after day, eaten together, gotten drunk together, basically not left each other's side the whole trip, and never even once did you mention that you would be studying at Cambridge after the holidays!

Nick knew all about my plans for the future, and several times I had told him about Trinity and how much I was looking forward to staying at one of the oldest colleges in town. I had actually grown very fond of him, and when he stood there in my room, with his charming smile, looking a bit flustered as if he had just happened to be passing by, I realised that I had missed him. Our friendship continued. We did a lot of things together in Cambridge, and I got to like him even more. And I often asked myself: why does he clam up as soon as things start to have to do with him and his own life? I cannot answer that. All I can say is – *typically Nick*.

A Poet with a Guitar

One night in February 1968 there is a knock at the door of Robert Kirby, a nineteen-year-old music student who lives in one of the old colleges in the heart of Cambridge.

Kirby – at that moment working on one of Debussy's compositions – puts down his sheet music and shuffles over to the door to answer. Outside, framed by the doorway, is a tall, brown-haired fellow with a guitar in his hand.

"He wanted to know if I could write arrangements for a couple of his songs," Kirby casually reports on this, his first meeting with Nick Drake. As his unexpected visitor settles down in the middle of the living room and strikes his first, inviting, catchy chords, it occurs to Kirby that he has seen this man before. "I was racking my brains, and then suddenly it hit me."

It was October 1967. Term had just begun when two first-year students, like so many other hopefuls, showed up for auditions for the university amateur theatrical club, The Footlights. The club's cabarets were a big deal in Cambridge and usually played to capacity crowds; if one got through the audition, there was a good chance of a career in show biz. Nick and Robert did not make it through.

"That was a bit awkward, of course," Kirby recalls. "We talked of anything but talent shows. And Nick kept strumming his guitar. After I heard two or three of his songs I accepted unconditionally."

During the next few days this student of classical music who is a specialist in orchestration begins to create arrangements for "Time of No Reply", "Magic", "Thoughts of Mary Jane", and "Day is Done".

"I had an old valve Ferrograph tape recorder which I used for the recordings, and not long after Nick showed up with new material. He was writing simple love songs. Personally I am very fond of this genre. And Nick's love songs were fabulous. One was called 'Blossom', another was called 'Rain' – which I scored for the French horn, you know *boob-boob-bob-bob*, which definitely didn't appeal to Nick's tastes. I had hours' worth of Nick Drake songs in all sorts of versions. Later I taped over all those reels with the work of other songwriters. I was a poor student, you know, and reel-to-reel tapes were expensive."

Robert Kirby smiles and shakes his head.

We are at the Youth Hostel in Holland Park, London, on a night in the spring of 2008. The busy arranger and producer has made his way through the pitch-dark park, and is now having a pint. He is cheerful and talkative, and I remark that he hasn't changed much. Robert is a well-rounded English gentleman, he is witty and articulate; often he cocks his head thoughtfully before answering a question. Details are important in these stories of his youth, in the same way that the violins are in a rock tune where the strings are not the main feature but have to be there to lend depth to the melody. It's been twenty-nine years since we last met. After my visit to Rodney and Molly's in November of 1979, I did an interview with Kirby, who then lived in a semi-detached house in Hampstead with his wife, kids, and cat. Strangely enough, that house was not far from Haverstock Hill where Nick was staying when he was working on the songs for *Bryter Layter*: "A corner house in the Victorian Gothic style," the arranger recalled. "Nick had two sparsely furnished rooms on the ground floor. I used to drop by all the time." Robert Kirby noticed that Nick had begun to isolate himself from the world, and that the house had been demolished a few years after he moved out.

None of us could possibly have known that the topic of our conversation then would end up becoming an icon on a par with Jim Morrison and Janis Joplin and other artists who got burned up by the cultural and musical Supernova of the sixties. A generation later, Kirby now talks about the impact Nick Drake's posthumous fame has had on his own career, and he dwells on how one, simple, apparently completely random, event can change a man's life.

In 1979 Kirby talked about his approach: "I tried to add to Nick's melodies an element of Impressionism because I was preoccupied with composers such as Ravel and Debussy. But during the recording of *Five Leaves Left* I realised that a song like 'Way to Blue' was much better off being handled as a Bach chorale. We kept only the strings and Nick's vocals. Therefore we discarded the guitar. The basic mood of the song somehow corresponded very well with that spiritual tone of the old masters. Nick loved the idea. Later I found out that his favourite composer was Johann Sebastian Bach."

♪♪♪

In a letter which Nick wrote to his parents right after meeting Robert Kirby, he characterised his friend in the following way: "He's rather a splendid fellow and looks rather like Haydn or Mozart or someone, being rather short and stocky with long, wavy hair and rimless spectacles. However he is quite hip to my sort of music, being quite a proficient folksinger himself."

In his teens Kirby had been part of a folk music group which toured Europe. When he first came to Cambridge he formed a pop group called The Gentle Power of Song, together with five of his fellow students. In the winter of '67 this band recorded a single and performed on the Christmas edition of *Dee Time*, the peak television pop programme on a Saturday night. Nick knew all that the night he knocked on Kirby's door in Gonville and Caius, at the heart of Cambridge. He was looking for an arranger who had experience within that broad range of genres which he himself was keen on: classical, folk, pop and rock. And Nick found what he was looking for. Robert Kirby was enthusiastic and he soon succeeded in recruiting a chamber orchestra among his fellow students. The songs began to take shape in their new arrangements. When summer came around all they needed to do was test them out on a live audience. And there was always an audience to be found at the 27 colleges in Cambridge. There were parties and concerts every weekend, not least the traditional May Balls (which, oddly enough, are always in June) and the graduation parties held by the students.

"We would be the act between the rock groups," Kirby tells me. "Nick would sit in the middle of the ensemble. He wore jeans and a black blazer; his guitar would rest on his crossed legs. In a semi-circle all around him the orchestra would fiddle away, all female musicians: violins, violas, cellos, and a single flute. Nick's guitar was perfectly tuned, and he never made any mistakes. He was quiet and shy and not at all the type who would tell jokes between songs. Still, he got along well with the audience. People simply liked his songs and the subtle way in which they were performed. These were small venues which rarely held more than a hundred and fifty people."

After the first few concerts a close friendship formed between Kirby and Drake. The two of them met in each other's rooms and discussed music, women, and other eternal mysteries, all the while sharing a joint.

"The first year Nick was staying at Fitzwilliam College outside town," Kirby recalls. "The walls of his room were plastered over with posters. He was selling these colourful Flower Power posters from San Francisco, not to make money but because it was a hip thing to do. His customers were flipped-out types from the university. Things were very happening back then. There was a constant feeling of rebellion in the air. And sometimes John Lennon and Yoko Ono would pop by for *surprise-gigs*, and we were all stoned, and the drugs were a part of the music and the music was a part of taking drugs; it was a way of being together, a new culture."

What was Nick like as a person? I asked Robert Kirby during our first interview in '79. The recording reveals a longish pause, ten, perhaps fifteen, seconds elapse where nothing comes. In the background the cat is mewing. Kirby clears his throat. Then he continues in a hesitant voice:

"In the circles we were frequenting I am sure there were people who considered him a little bit arrogant. I remember visiting him at his parents' house in Tanworth, where their house stood in large grounds. Inside I was received by their Burmese housemaid who politely took my coat. I knew that his father was a managing director and that his sister Gabrielle was a famous actress. I should add here that I come from a working class family. I've always had to work hard to get scholarships so that I could continue my studies. In other words, there was a glaring contrast between Nick's family background and my own, but I never felt that it had any impact on our friendship whatsoever. Nick was a person who reflected on things, very much interested in his surroundings. At the same time he had a good sense of irony. Seen in the light of the heavy depression that later cast a shadow over his life, it may sound paradoxical to mention this, but I always found Nick an easy person to be together with. When we had finished a concert we would go to pubs and have a few pints. We would look at the ladies, and talk about all and sundry. It was rare for us to get into any deep conversations. We were a couple of young students. We were happy with what we were doing and we enjoyed each other's company."

"One day he came by and played me a song he had just written. It was 'Fruit Tree'. We were talking about how to arrange this beautiful ballad. Nick obviously had doubts. 'Oboes – or strings, maybe...' he mumbled, only to interrupt himself. 'But that is your job, right?' In other words, he was giving me a free hand, and that felt like a privilege. Considering how ambitious he was, one *had* to do one's absolute best. Nick was very meticulous with his lyrics, the sound of the words and the rhymes, you know. If a line sounded too heavy-handed or unambiguous he would get rid of it. The poetry of it was what mattered to him. What his songs were all about was up to people themselves to find out."

Nick hadn't made the cut with The Footlights, but what was worse, he had been given digs at a college which was nothing like he had imagined Cambridge to be – the university assigning colleges to students who put in an open application, without specifying a college of their choice. He, the engineer's son, had passed his entry exams. He had got into one of the finest universities in England, and was now about to reside at this stronghold of education, he thought, in a city full of bridges and parks, gardens and crooked streets where all the old colleges rise like fairytale castles by the river Cam. He had imagined himself in a room with a view. Nice and cosy chambers by the river – at Trinity, for instance, where Richard his fellow-traveller from Morocco held court, or, even better, they could have put him at Gonville and Caius where he had a friend who was reading English as he was. The Faculty of English was next door to Caius. Why, then, had they put him a mile away from the centre of things?

Fitzwilliam College opened in 1966.

Its long dark halls spread like office buildings on a field north of town. In the middle sits a square building with a strange copper roof, which makes one think of a Buddhist temple; this is the college Dining Hall where Nick is expected to show up for breakfast and dinner. When he has been out with his friends till all hours getting drunk, which happens now and then, he has to prepare himself for a long walk up the Huntingdon Road. Uphill. All the way.

Nick quickly realises he has to adapt to two unfortunate circumstances. The rooms at Fitzwilliam are built for pygmies. In fact, even midgets would have a hard time squeezing into these fifty square feet. There is just room for a bed, a chair, and a table in the rectangular room, which – possibly because the architect was ashamed of himself for drawing up plans for a student flat the size of a jail cell – has one window fully as big as the wall itself. For Nick, who lives on the ground floor, this means that everyone outside in the courtyard can see everything he is up to. Unless he keeps his curtains drawn. But who wants to keep his curtains drawn on a sunny day, or on a grey one for that matter, when you need each and every ray of light in the world? He has stacks of books to get through. Blake, Stevenson, and Dickens, English Romantic literature, all part of the first term syllabus. He has to stash his guitar under the bed. Every time he feels a spark of inspiration he has to get down on all fours and crawl around like a dog, twisting himself so as to avoid making a scratch in the varnish or denting the case.

The other unfortunate fact: all the students wearing suits and ties, coming and going around the college, the newcomers, and his next-door neighbours – virtually all of them have *short hair*. They look like rugby players to Nick. They look like lawyers and book-keepers, civil servants and secretaries in dreary ministries, and he begins to realise that even the fairy castles are breeding grounds for worker bees who – as soon as their wings will carry them, and their youth has passed by like one side of a Doors record – fly off into the bustling hive of society, find their set places in the hierarchies, and buzz around in cells not much bigger than the ones at Fitzwilliam College. Of course, some end up with a large fancy office. Some advance; others are kept down. And he sees how absurd this whole construction is, and that it doesn't matter whether you are inside or out, whether you reach the top or hit the bottom:

When the day is done
Down to earth then sinks the sun
Along with everything that was lost and won
When the day is done.

But it is not until later, when Nick has left Fitzwilliam and moved into a house by the river, that he writes this song about the futility of life. We are still in October '67, freshman orientation has just begun, and all the new students at the Faculty of English – across from Caius, the medieval college – are trying to learn each other's names while antiquated professors wearing capes and mortar boards introduce the syllabus for November and December. The colleges have ancient traditions meant to bring the students together. These are the Societies. There are a myriad different ones, where the young have a chance to pursue their interests, from croquet to Karl Marx, from chess to Shakespeare: in short, whatever takes their fancy. Names such as The Boat Club, The Cricket Club, The Cross-Country Club, and The Rowing Society reveal that extra-curricular activities are high on the agenda of Cambridge students.

As for Nick, he is inducted as 'the Odde Fellow' into The Loungers, a society where people meet to eat breakfast together and, according to a former member, folk singer Paul Wheeler, do as little as possible. Despite its roots back in the sixteenth century The Loungers are *anti-establishment*, just like The Buddhist Society.

The members of The Buddhist Society are long-haired, pot-smoking, haiku-reading chaps. They don't ride around on bicycles as the fellows in the sports clubs do; they go by foot, and they have all the time in the world.

The members of The Buddhist Society listen to The Grateful Dead and read Jack Kerouac. They are the local Dharma Bums. Nick shows up at the club meetings in black, he is elegant and suave, a dandy with shoulder-length hair and a fag dangling from the corner of his mouth. But behind all his coolness he is open and sensitive.

Zen Buddhism is an anti-philosophy which suits a young intellectual who has already internalised the works of Sartre and Nietzsche and has spent many an hour studying the quintessential twentieth-century philosophy, existentialism. Nick has no trouble connecting Zen with his favourite poet William Blake, the mystic, the body of whose work is a protest against the material illusion of the world. Man is the Poetical Genius, says Blake. All is emptiness, says Zen. *Won't you come and say if you know the way to blue,* says Nick after reading the Bhagavad-Gita, or was it Allen Ginsberg? The poem becomes one of the first songs which seems successful to the hypercritical nineteen-year-old. He is looking for that "other"; call it "enlightenment", "God", or a "reality behind reality".

The journey is the end, and the end is the journey.

Nick is on a journey into himself.

In The Buddhist Society he meets another Caius student named Peter Russell who introduces him to Transcendental Meditation. The two friends sign up for a course in this form of meditation, founded by an Indian, Maharishi Mahesh Yogi, in 1957, on the threshold of consumer society. Ten years on, the Yogi includes George

Harrison and John Lennon among his students. The spiritual insights which TM offers do not come for free. The students buy a mantra personal to each and whispered into their ears by the guide on the last day of Step 1. This takes place during a ceremony where the student brings flowers and a towel, kneels down, and listens to a series of prayers which the guide makes a point of explaining have nothing to do with religion, but are just part of the technique, also known as The Rapid Road to the Deep Rest. The Mantra is a secret. If you reveal it to anyone else, it loses its power.

Like so many others who learn TM, Nick is enthusiastic about meditation for a month or two and then he gives it up altogether. He doesn't have time to sit down with his eyes closed twice a day for twenty minutes and repeat a sound that rhymes with AM or ING. He settles for putting The Moody Blues on his turntable. The acid prophets' new album, *In Search of the Lost Chord*, fades away with flute and sitar, and a male choir humming the mantra of the universe: OM.

⫶

"*The hippie culture? The alternative society?*"

Robert Kirby sits and fiddles a bit with the label of his green beer bottle and lets his mind wander. "Well, you could put it this way: we were both in and out. We were musicians first and foremost. And yes, we did smoke pot. There was nothing odd about that; all our friends did the same thing. We smoked a joint when we went out for an evening. We smoked at parties and when we went punting on the river. But I can't recall us ever getting wasted like a couple of heroin addicts. In fact I never saw Nick do any hard drugs."

"Sometimes he seemed depressed," Kirby continues. "Many of us were. At twenty you sometimes feel a bit world-weary. One day you are up, the next you are as low as you can get. I have to say it as it is. In Cambridge I never thought of Nick as mentally ill. He was not ordinary, though. He was different."

His parents write long letters to him. Rodney, especially, is worried about the somewhat erratic communications from Fitzwilliam College. He impresses on his son that he must follow classes. Nick replies: "All I care about is playing and singing."

And while it is true that Nick is modest by nature, according to Robert Kirby it would be as inaccurate to characterise him as a "tortured artist" as it would be to dismiss Paul McCartney as a "happy lad from Liverpool." Quite the contrary, Nick is extremely extroverted. He continues his style from Marlborough and does all he can to get to perform. He plays at parties and student gatherings, meets new people, writes new songs, and he is occasionally invited to give a concert at a pub, a folk music club, or venues such as Lady Mitchell Hall, one of the largest lecture theatres at Cambridge University. And he loves it.

"It may surprise you to hear that during the last few weeks I have been extraordinarily happy with life and I haven't a clue why," he writes to his parents. "It seems that Cambridge in fact can do very nice things to one if one lets it. And I'm not sure that I did let it before. I think I have thrown one or two rather useless and restrictive complexes that I had picked up before coming here. This seems to have become rather self-indulgent and boring so I'll stop."

One night in November Nick stands at the bar of The Criterion by the market square. Over the last few months this traditional pub has become the gathering place of choice for political activists, folk musicians, and members of the more obscure student societies. It's nearly eleven. Young men in flowery shirts, headbands, and hair as impressive as any Indian chief are sitting around tables, next to elderly, well-dressed gentlemen. There is a busy flow of people in and out of the pub. Inside, the dominant smell is the sweet scent of Virginia tobacco; outside in the back alley it smells of resin as in a Swedish pine forest.

"Last orders!" the barkeeper calls out.

Nick glances around the room. He has been waiting for an hour or so for a few of his new friends to show up. He shakes himself, tries to bring himself to step outside in the cold. Just as he has finished putting his overcoat on and emptied his glass, he turns to the bar.

"Excuse me, do you have a piece of paper?"

"Paper?" the barkeeper says. "Will a napkin do?"

"All right, sure," Nick says. "And a pencil, too?"

The barman smirks.

"Did you suddenly remember her phone number here at last call?"

"Yes, something like that," Nick mumbles.

The bartender slides a napkin and a pen over the counter.

"Thanks a lot."

Nick scratches his head and stands for a while, staring absent-mindedly into the clouds of smoke. Then he scribbles four words. Whereupon he strides purposefully out of the bar, clearly uplifted, even with a secretive smile playing around his lips.

Sometimes, it is so simple.

A punch line, a sudden idea: four words and the rest follow automatically. Other times, nothing comes. It is as if the words die while crossing the short distance from hand to paper, and he knows the moment he writes them down that they are dead.

What came first, the melody or the lyrics, the chicken or the egg?

In Nick's case: both.

Often he has a riff, but no words. And just as often he has the words but no riff.

He is a guitarist who writes poems.

A poet with a guitar.

The light is on in one of the ground floor rooms at Fitzwilliam College. Nick is sitting on his bed with his guitar in his lap, between stacks of books and piles of dirty laundry. Every now and then he gets up and goes over to the table to write. With pen and black ink. In front of him lies a napkin with four words scribbled on it.

The table is overflowing with papers. He lights a cigarette, forgets all about it, writes a few sentences, strikes them out, starts all over again; next to the ashtray he has a cup of coffee from the morning from which he occasionally takes a sip. Nick touches the strings of his guitar softly with the flat of his hand so as not to disturb his neighbours, hums the verses and the chorus over and over again, chasing the melody, chasing the words as the hours slip by without a trace like cigarette smoke. When he falls into bed at sunrise, he is exhausted and he does not set his alarm clock.

The American

London, spring 1968. The protests against America's war in Vietnam culminate on 17 March, when thousands of demonstrators clash with riot police and mounted police in front of the American Embassy in Grosvenor Square, Mayfair. Anarchists, communists, peace activists, and members of the student movement, all come together in one great mosaic, waving red flags and banners with anti-American slogans; genteel Mayfair resounds with chants of *Ho-Ho-Ho-Chi-Minh* on this Sunday afternoon. As the parade streams into the square the first demonstrators start throwing cobblestones at the embassy. The police attack the crowd with their truncheons, and what was meant to be a peace demonstration quickly devolves into a giant, disorganised brawl.

There is unrest in the capital. A new generation is manifesting itself, in its own language. Not everyone is jumping onto the barricades. We find the youth of London everywhere, flocking to the basements and garages; we find them in side-street pubs, Soho clubs, and all around the suburbs where they channel their visions of change through hundred-watt amplifiers. They have week-long sessions where all the dreamers and lost troubadours can work through their aggression and contempt for the entire establishment.

A few months before the Grosvenor Square riots, an event has taken place that turns young songwriter Nick Drake's life upside down once and for all. In The

Roundhouse, one of the underground venues where a group of disillusioned architecture students calling themselves Pink Floyd perform on a regular basis, there is a charity event.

Here in the circular concert venue in Chalk Farm, near Hampstead, the Vietnam Committee have booked five days in December to present a number of hot acts from the US and England, among which we find Country Joe and the Fish, and Fairport Convention.

After Fairport's concert the bassist Ashley "Tyger" Hutchings hangs around to listen to the other bands perform: "I was wandering around the inner perimeters when I heard a sound from way up the stage which struck me, forcibly. It was unlike anything I had heard during the day. There was no light show, no rock guitar solos; there was just this guy playing his songs. What hit me more than anything was his presence. He had an enormous charisma, even though he barely moved on stage."

It's two o'clock in the morning and Ashley Hutchings is really on his way home. But when the unknown guitarist leaves the stage, Hutchings follows him and asks him for his phone number. The guitarist seems impressed to be sought out by a member of Fairport Convention. He explains that he comes from Cambridge where he is reading English and that the festival committee has given him ten minutes to present his songs.

"Would you like to become a professional musician?" Hutchings asks him.

"Yes, that's my plan," the guitarist admits.

"Rich and famous?" Hutchings laughs.

"Exactly," the guitarist replies.

"Good," Hutchings says, "I'll see what I can do."

A few days later Nick gets a call from Fairport's producer, Joe Boyd. He asks Nick if he would like to stop by with a few demos of his songs.

"Uhm, all right," Nick says, amazed. "When would you want me to do that?"

"Bring it to my office tomorrow morning," Boyd says.

Nick has a lot of tapes with demos; all recorded on Robert Kirby's old Ferrograph in his room at Gonville and Caius. Just voice and guitar – simple recordings used by the two friends to arrange Nick's songs for concerts.

♪♪♪

In his musical memoir, *White Bicycles*, Joe Boyd recounts his meeting with the young songwriter that day in Charlotte Street, London, where Nick turned up at his office "in a black wool overcoat stained with cigarette ash."

> *He was tall and handsome with an apologetic stoop;*
> *either he had no idea how good looking he was or was*
> *embarrassed by the fact. He handed me the tape and*
> *shuffled out the door.*[3]

On the label is written in black ink: "Magic", "Time has Told Me", and "Thoughts of Mary Jane".

Later that day Joe Boyd takes the time to listen to the songs. He puts the reel-to-reel tape on the machine he has in his office, leans back in his chair and readies himself for what he fully expects to be one of the usual Bob Dylan or Paul Simon clones. An acoustic guitar rings like a bell

---

3   *White Bicycles* (London: Serpent's Tail, 2006), p. 191.

through the room. The voice, which is interlaced between the notes, discreetly, as if part of the jangle of the strings, makes the gangly long-haired American take his feet off the desk and sit up straight. For the next few minutes he is quite flabbergasted. He sits and wonders where the hell he has heard these melodies before, but he can't come up with anything.

There are some obvious affinities between the nineteen-year-old songwriter and his future producer. Both men are over six foot three. Both are slim and handsome, with elegant articulate movements. They are both observers and perfectionists. In other areas, however, Drake and Boyd are as different as night and day.

By the time Joe Boyd meets Nick Drake at his office in the smart London neighbourhood of Marylebone that day in January 1968, the American has had a fast and wide-flung career taking him through virtually every music scene in the Western hemisphere. He has toured the US and Europe with the top names in jazz, blues, and soul – acts such as Coleman Hawkins, Muddy Waters, and Sister Rosetta Tharpe. He was one of the prime movers behind the Newport Folk Festival in 1965, and ran the sound-board the night Bob Dylan shocked the world of protest-singers and folk music enthusiasts by playing the electric guitar, backed by the Paul Butterfield Blues Band.

By the end of that very year Joe Boyd and one of his friends, John Hopkins, establish the UFO Club, the most important underground venue in all London. The American is always keeping his ears and eyes open for talent from the traditional British folk scene. In 1967 he produces the breakthrough album by The Incredible String Band, *The 5000 Spirits or the Layers of Onions* – the quintessential hippie album – and Pink Floyd's debut single, *Arnold Layne*, one of the weirdest pop songs in rock history, with its story of a transvestite who runs around at night stealing underwear from people's clothes lines. The song receives the distinction of being banned from several national radio stations. Before the age of twenty-five, Harvard student Joe, this soldier of fortune from Princeton, New Jersey, will have created his own sound, a *sound of surprise*, which almost preternaturally combines the traditional instruments of folk music with the new tones of psychedelic rock.

Boyd is instantly keen to record the shy Englishman. His plan is to create string arrangements for Nick's songs. The inspiration comes from Canadian poet Leonard Cohen whose debut LP has just landed in college digs and student apartments all over the world. Cohen recites his love poems over a string accompaniment, dry and cool with little to add to his deep nasal tones other than female back-up singers. The album becomes a massive hit.

Nick has already introduced *Songs of Leonard Cohen* to his close university friend, Brian Wells, and the idea of orchestral strings appeals to him. "He described performing with a string quartet at a Cambridge May Ball," Joe Boyd recalls. "That was the first moment of our meeting when he became animated."[4]

Boyd's next thought is: how do I get a hold of the best arranger in England? He calls up The Beatles' record company and is put in touch with one of Paul McCartney's friends, Richard Hewson, a classically trained musician and Apple staff arranger. Hewson is sent the tape with

4   *White Bicycles*, p. 192

Nick's three songs and accepts the job. Hewson was behind the arrangements for James Taylor's first LP and has just put the finishing touches to "Those were the Days" with a young singer called Mary Hopkin. To get an idea of the Drake–Hewson combination, this Russian folk melody encapsulated by Hewson in 1001 strings – the summer hit of 1968 – may give you a clue.

One morning Boyd meets up with his regular sound man John Wood in the Sound Techniques Studio. The American has booked a chamber orchestra to test out Richard Hewson's arrangements. The orchestra arrives and Nick shows up with his guitar. It is perfectly tuned and he plays the songs without any mistakes, makes his way through "Magic", "Day is Done", and "Thoughts of Mary Jane" while the orchestra do their best to follow. When Nick and Joe afterwards listen through the recordings, they agree that it does not work. There's too much distance between Nick's voice and the guitar-playing and these splendid, but slightly anonymous arrangements, it seems like they move in opposite directions.

What now?

To Boyd's surprise Nick starts talking about a guy in Cambridge who already *had* done arrangements for the songs. And who is he? The producer wants to know. One of my fellow students, Nick explains. Joe Boyd is not wildly impressed. But after some consideration he agrees to give the project a chance. The following week he and Nick drive up to Cambridge to meet Robert Kirby.

What Exactly is a Dream?

The English music scene of early 1969 is a boiling cauldron in which musical styles, instruments, and human voices mix and meld together into all manner of new forms. With *Rubber Soul, Revolver,* and *Sgt. Pepper's Lonely Hearts Club Band,* The Beatles have set a whole new standard for ways of creating songs. The Liverpool quartet don't just smoke pot and drop LSD, they sing about it, let the drugs colour the meter and the rhyme so that the band's happy-go-lucky and seemingly harmless pop songs suddenly become deeply ambiguous, causing millions of teenagers to become textual interpreters.

In 1969, hallucinogenic drugs have become an integral part of youth culture. The musicians are stoned and so is the audience.

Turn on, tune in, drop out, runs the slogan of Timothy Leary, psychologist and former professor at Harvard University, now the standard-bearer of the hippie movement and a self-proclaimed "visionary prophet".

Come together/Right now/Over me, sings John Lennon. This song opens the new Beatles album *Abbey Road* and is written at the request of Dr. Leary, after the LSD guru and his wife spend 24 hours with John and Yoko at a bed-in for peace in Montreal.

Brian Jones is found dead at the bottom of his swimming pool on the night between 2nd and 3rd July, pumped full of drugs; Syd Barrett is committed to a mental institution; Jimi Hendrix looks more and more like a walking ghost, and still no warning lights go off in the branch of show biz called psychedelic or progressive rock. On the contrary there is a feeling of being on the eve of a revolution, anything can happen, anything goes as long as the music keeps playing and the vibes are good.

New and advanced recording techniques, the Mellotron and other instruments, happenings and festivals such as Woodstock and the Isle of Wight, the openness of the times, an optimism carried by the warm winds of the economic upturn – all this and more seems to put a number of very different musicians in an ideal situation with regard to expressive and artistic freedom.

The flagship of the underground scene, Pink Floyd – who have just lost their lead singer, the previously mentioned Syd Barrett – enter the studio during the spring and emerge from it with a double album, *Umma Gumma*, a series of wildly experimental, psychedelic, midnight ceremonies for drums, organ, and guitar. At any moment the music can break down into a cacophony of noise, just as when Hendrix explodes on his Stratocaster in an orgy of over- and undertones out of which a weird and heartrending beauty rises from the ashes like a phoenix.

The LP is the medium of the generation; liberation from authority of any kind is one of the aims. The key aim. The one that drowns out everything else. The songs get longer and longer, as do the hair of the guitarists and the solos they perform. Simultaneously, as an obvious and natural part of the liberation, the youth of London listen to Tamla Motown, because the youngsters demand the right to dance and crave a constant quota of three-minute pop songs that pull a bit of heaven down to earth.

As for rhythm and blues, this traditionally black style

– adopted by The Rolling Stones and other prominent white bands – has been given a shot of Celtic mysticism by the Irish singer Van Morrison and his groovy improvisations on *Astral Weeks*, an album we later discover in Nick Drake's record collection; perhaps the most worn-out of them all.

And folk music goes to rock, jazz goes to rock, gospel and soul go to rock, and rock itself goes everywhere.

On to the stage flock a multitude of bands: Fairport Convention, Pentangle, Jethro Tull, Led Zeppelin, and Free, to mention but a few; bands with their roots in skiffle and shuffle and boogie and blues, as well as groups that spring out of the classical music programmes of the universities. Their message? Often just a play on words. But just as often a rebellion against king and country; a storm of laughter, screams, and cries – electric emergency signals from a generation trying to find its feet in the midst of all the changes. Behind the bubbly surface there is a desperation lurking, which strikes down fragile souls like the head of an axe.

See me/Feel me/Touch me, The Who sing in their rock opera *Tommy*, putting into words this feeling that runs like an undercurrent through a part of this generation: the sense of *not* being seen, of *not* being heard.

And acid head Syd Barrett leaves the mental institution and goes home to Cambridge to study the Irish poet James Joyce, stuffs himself with LSD, and once again climbs into his quiet nocturnal mineshafts to explore the question *What exactly is a dream?* – the last line of the last record Barrett did with Pink Floyd.

Over the summer a new voice emerges on the English music scene. That of a young poet and guitarist who does nothing to promote himself; he just shows up with his songs, relying on a few solitary record buyers to discover his existence. His name is Nick Drake. His debut album is difficult to categorise by standard musical parameters. It is not folk or rock, nor is it blues or jazz, but rather a sum of all the parts: folk-rock-blues-jazz – with the addition of a string ensemble. Not a word about politics. No emotionally charged protests against war and capitalism. On the contrary: Lifeblood. *Weltschmerz*. An emotional, dark poetry. This is how Nick Drake gives a new lease of life to the ailing singer-songwriter tradition in the decade about to begin.

⋏⋇⋇

Nick's forthcoming album is called *Saturday Sun*; a title which nods in the direction of two of his favourites, Tim Buckley's *Goodbye and Hello* and Van Morrison's *Astral Weeks*. The title is short, pithy, and poetic. In addition, "Saturday Sun" is one of the last songs he has written; it is the last song on the record and in a certain way embodies the essence of the album. His friends like the title. But the more he thinks about it, the more doubts he has. Is "Saturday Sun" truly a headline that ties the ten very different compositions together? He has spent a year recording the album. He has changed the arrangements, worked hard on the melodies and lyrics, and along the way he has discarded a number of songs that were good enough on their own, but for some reason did not complement the whole. The problem with the title is that it closes in on itself. The words *Saturday* and *sun* have positive connotations. Not until you listen to the track do you understand the irony; that it is precisely about not enjoying the sunshine on your day off but, on the contrary, about the vacuum the weekend leaves you in.

The songs have all been mixed and the cover is ready for the printer when, one night in his bedsit on Carlyle Road, Cambridge, he settles down to look at some photos. They have been taken by a fellow called Keith Morris; a friend of Joe Boyd's and connected with the manager's production company, Witchseason.

Nick had met the photographer one afternoon in April. Morris had been assigned to do the press shoot and cover photo. They spend a few hours driving around various locations in London. Nick poses for Keith's reflex camera in an overgrown garden and in the attic of an old, abandoned house. Normally he doesn't enjoy having his picture taken. But Morris is a funny guy. Very down to earth and relaxed, an anarchist in his approach to the world; what's more, the man takes an interest in poetry. They are on the same wavelength right from the start. They agree that Nick should try to avoid smiling. So, none of the usual *say cheese*, but rather *stay cool*. That is surprisingly easy, although on several occasions he has a hard time keeping a straight face.

Nick moves his little brass lamp around, spreads the photographs on the table in front of him, and carefully studies the three or four prospects for the sleeve. The best ones are those taken in Battersea, he thinks. The snapshots of him leaning against a wall as people rush by, on their way home from work. This is how he would like to be represented, in full figure, casually leaning back, and – yes please – with the world at arm's length. Other shots show the sensitive side of Nick; yet others show Nick as a philosopher, the poet with his face in the half-light. Each and every one of these photos is true and uncovers a side of his personality that he can fully endorse.

Then there are the pictures that didn't make the final cut. He runs through that pile, stops and dwells on one that Mum and Dad would surely love. Keith Morris has caught him with a big smile, his eyes shining with sincere, naïve joy. There is no hiding that this is basically an optimistic person. The picture tells a story. Here is a college boy who has scored a record deal and who has just completed a masterpiece. He believes in his project, he believes in the future. If he could just come up with a better title, the situation would be nearly perfect.

It is after midnight. The window on the garden is open; when he sits perfectly still he can hear the ripple of the river like some faraway music. The night air smells of soil and freshly cut grass. The willow tree with freshly opened buds stands like a veil in the dark, a big, beautiful living organism in the middle of the deserted garden.

One last cigarette before bed.

Nick fishes his tobacco and rolling papers out of his shirt pocket, fumbles with the tobacco, opens the red packet of papers and pulls out a little slip: "Five leaves left." He has done this a hundred times before. Running out of paper is a routine occurrence for roll-up smokers. As he puts the slip down among Keith Morris' photos something unexpected happens. He suddenly realises what the slip says. He bends forward and stares at the three words, tastes them, speaks them out loud and clear, whereupon he sits up straight and sees his face in the dark mirror of the window pane.

Nick smiles.

The first track on the album is about love. We are a far cry from the genre of "simple love songs." Nick actually wrote such songs and ended up ditching them; "Time has Told Me" tells you why in four minutes. He wants to go somewhere else. By juxtaposing complex emotions with images of mystical, poetic force, he hits a place where love transcends, a place where love becomes a road to personal liberation:

Time has told me
You're a rare, rare find
A troubled cure
For a troubled mind.

This catchy blues is played in waltz time. Nick's solid, basic chords are complemented and extended by Danny Thompson's improvisations on the bass and Richard Thompson's rolling country guitar, while the singer sends his voiced Ss sliding up and down the melody. He sounds hopeful. As if he puts his trust in the formula repeated in the chorus: *Someday our ocean/Will find its shore.*

According to his fellow student, guitarist Paul Wheeler, the line "time has told me" came to Nick in a late evening hour at the bar of The Footlights. That was shortly after he started university. Rodney and Molly remember the song as one of the first that he wrote after the time in Aix-en-Provence and hint that it is directly addressed to a girl he met in Cambridge. "He didn't say a thing to us about her, but it was clear that he was head over heels in love with her."

In October of 1968 Nick leaves his digs at Fitzwilliam College, all according to plan. He has finished his freshman year at The Faculty of English.

Paul Wheeler used to meet with Nick several times a week that autumn. The two of them would jam on each other's compositions, and one of the first things Nick would do when he had written a new song was present it to his friend, the folk musician.

"He moved into a room near by the river," Wheeler recounts. "The house was outside the town centre as such, which meant that he had to cross one of the old bridges every day on his way to and from the university. He would often stop and watch the currents and the leaves floating by. I know that 'River Man' is a portrait of the situation Nick found himself in, both geographically and emotionally."

The song came with the river. And just as the river comes from a modest spring in a field or from behind a shrubbery on a hillside, the song begins almost obscurely and then grows into a flowing stream. First a few jazz chords, then the bass trickles in, then the vocals, then the violins, the rhythm constantly the same, gliding, flowing, but the currents shift – now lazy, now hasty; the course of the river through the landscape.

In the song the narrator has a visit from a friend:

Betty came by on her way
Said she had a word to say
About things today
And fallen leaves.
. . .

Betty said she prayed today
For the sky to blow away

Or maybe stay
She wasn't sure.

Business as usual. The state of the world. One human being's doubts, prayers, hopes. The time goes by, and suddenly the leaves fall and it is autumn. The river man knows all this; he is time itself and outside time; he reflects the life that goes by, the clouds, the rain, the people, this whole fleeting shadowplay; he changes colour with the surroundings and yet remains unchanging, the same, as emphasised in the last line of the song, in the refrain *Oh, how they come and go*.

Here we hear the member of The Buddhist Society, the poet and Taoist talking. A way of opening "River Man" could easily be through Chuang Tzu, the Chinese sage who was born in the fourth century BC and a Taoist before such a rubric existed.

In a slight re-write of Chuang Tzu's story *The Butterfly Dream* one could say that Nick once dreamed that he was a river. He flowed along without a care and didn't think of anything other than being a river. Then, suddenly, he wakes up and realises that he is Nick. But now he doesn't know if he is Nick who dreamed that he was a river, or if he really is a river dreaming that it is Nick.

And of course there is the guitar, Nick's guitar; six strings that beat like a restless heart through the spacious compositions.

"His style was unique," Paul Wheeler claims. "Actually I have never heard anyone play anything like the way Nick handled some of his songs. Listen to Robert Johnson, for instance, and you'll discover that a lot of guitarists have learned a lot from him over the years. But as far as I know no one has tried to imitate Nick. Why? Perhaps because it is so damned hard. You can easily rack your brain for a couple of days trying to figure out what tuning the man has used. And the tuning changes from song to song."

This special method of tuning a high string a tone or two below a low string, and vice versa, is the secret behind Nick's guitar melodies. Most the beautiful and odd sequences he squeezes out of his instrument spring from these *strange tunings*.

In "Fruit Tree" he philosophises about the fact that the world is as blind as an old horse and that great artists often die before their time, in poverty, unrecognised for what they are, as happened to William Blake, Edgar Allan Poe, Franz Schubert, van Gogh, and Kafka, to mention but a few in the endless list of masters who did not live to reap the fruits of their labour.

They'll all know/That you were here/When you're gone, Nick ends. With a sigh of resignation. As if he – at the age of nineteen – already knows that he will never live long enough to get through to his audience, be heard, understood, recognised, or at least just accepted by the people his songs are addressed to. Which means, first and foremost, the rebels, the bohemians, the dreamers, all the night-hawks in all the backstreet bars in London, Tangier, Aix-en-Provence; the poets, dressed in black, rambling down the streets with verses written on napkins tucked away in their coat pockets.

Three hours from sundown
Jeremy flies
Hoping to keep
The sun from his eyes
East from the city
And down to the cave
In search of a master
In search of a slave.

These are the words somewhere in between the exotic conga drums on the track "Three Hours". This song is inspired by Jeremy Mason, Nick's schoolfriend who, besides his appetite for literature, also has quite a bit of Casanova about him (in the second verse of the song, Casanova's first name Jacomo is used). Jeremy is a ladies' man, forever chasing erotic adventures, and Nick quickly realises what the game is about. To seek satisfaction for one's bodily needs is a game that involves hidden feelings; behind the tricks of the seducer and the sweetness of the act of love-making is a longing for communion with another human being. Pain is Casanova's constant companion. The moment he has caught his prey, he loses interest in it.

Perhaps the secret of Nick's songs is that they are all written *"three hours from speaking."* In absolute silence. In an extraordinary emptiness. Personally, he hangs on to a dream of the romantic landscapes of a lost era, or he dives into the byways of his unconscious mind, looking for a lost identity, only to surface between the sailing violins of "Way to Blue" and wonder about the many ways of the light.

Can you understand the light among the trees? he asks with sincerity in his voice, like that of a young child who takes his first walk through a green forest with his mother.

Nick asks so many strange questions and generally allows himself to be swallowed up by mysteries that few would even bother to contemplate.

And the more he sees, the less he understands.

Perhaps because there is no one who really understands him.

Listen to "Saturday Sun", the track that originally should have lent its name to the whole album.

"Saturday Sun" tells the whole story.

To begin with, the song resembles a simple ode to the sun floating in a cloudless, blue sky early one morning. A song of praise to the golden rays that bring the world into our room. But no. Before Nick has even opened his shutters the Saturday sun has turned to Sunday's rain. Day is done, and what it brought was just a repeat of yesterday's rituals. One can almost see this tall man shrug his shoulders during the repetitive refrain *again and again*.

Just rain, pouring rain, all day long.

And nothing-new-under-the-sun.

So Sunday sat in the Saturday sun
And wept for a day gone by.

One could cry an ocean of salty tears for all this *tristesse*, if it weren't for the arrangement and the sophisticated, jazzy tune which carries "Saturday Sun". A piano *à la* Oscar Peterson's "Hymn to Freedom", bouncy, soaring, the light cling-clang of a vibraphone, and in the background a pair of cat's paws on a high hat: this is how the melancholia is constantly lightened.

What exactly is a dream?

This is the question one is forced to pose when listening

to *Five Leaves Left*. It is as if Nick is approaching the anatomy of a dream in these songs; as if he is teasing secrets out of his unconscious mind which he discreetly shares with us as the music plays – even if some passages can seem farther out, as strange and unreal as a dream *within* a dream.

The feeling of being left with a blank is unique.

To penetrate the flickering and constantly shifting atmosphere of *Five Leaves Left* is in some ways like waking up in a faraway place. Waking up in a house free of people. The walls are made of wood. You rummage through the drawers and cupboards, find a stack of letters tied with a silk ribbon, an old newspaper, a few sea shells. Outside, the wind is sighing in the pines. The sun is sinking low. You seem to have been here before. But you have forgotten when and why.

> *Think about stories with reason and rhyme*
> *Circling through your brain.*

Notice how Nick doesn't sing. He spins or hums – like a pair of insect wings buzzing.

His voice surfaces casually among the strings, elegant, as if it were an integral part of the cello group; it never breaks, never becomes shrill, hollow, or whiny – on the contrary it maintains, even in very sombre passages, a hovering, casually floating quality. Nor is there any trace of aggression or irony, but openness. A familiarity and confidentiality in the tone that springs from the close address of his voice to the listener. Dare one call it sensual, and instantly add that the magical aspect of it could possibly be founded on something akin to a volcano of unresolved sexual tensions, which still somehow dissolve the moment Nick touches his strings. It is not a sexy voice. But still it oozes a fine and mild eroticism.

The Royal Festival Hall

Five Leaves Left is released in the hectic mid-summer of 1969, just as the US is putting the first man on the moon.

On 26 July, *Melody Maker* has a small note about the record, in which Nick Drake's debut album is called "poetic" and "interesting." In August Nick performs three songs on John Peel's live broadcast on Radio 1, drawing listeners mostly from the London area. And then silence. He is not in demand from any other radio or TV stations. As for *Oz*, this influential music magazine carries no review of the record at all.

When the recordings for *Five Leaves Left* began in June of the previous year, Joe Boyd secured a contract for his artist with Island Records, a small record company with a solid reputation, which had specialised in music from Jamaica and had taught the English to dance to ska and blue beat. Jimmy Cliff was among the emerging Island acts, as were progressive white bands such as Traffic and Jethro Tull.

The founder of Island, Chris Blackwell, likes *Five Leaves Left*. All six employees at Joe Boyd's production company Witchseason are crazy about the record. But in spite of Blackwell's enthusiasm and Boyd's ability to bring together the right people at the right time, they do not succeed in generating attention for the 21-year-old songwriting talent from Cambridge. However, Joe Boyd has an idea up his sleeve. He has just finished production on the fourth Fairport Convention album, *Liege and Lief*, which is already rumoured to be a milestone in folk rock history, prior to its actual release. To celebrate this event Boyd hires The Royal Festival Hall, one of London's foremost performance venues, which lies facing the Thames between Waterloo Bridge and Westminster Bridge.

At nine o'clock on the evening of Wednesday 24 September, a stooped and rather pale-looking Nick Drake enters the concert hall, carrying his guitar. Joe Boyd gives a brief and slightly nervous introduction for the audience. Nick sits on a stool in the middle of the stage, silent, strikes a couple of chords; he is blinking into the sharp light of the projectors, trying to get used to their glare. The Royal Festival Hall is abuzz with voices. It is nearly sold out. John and Beverly Martyn have just left the stage; now there is an audience of nearly three thousand people waiting for tonight's high point, Fairport Convention, fronted by Sandy Denny on vocals and the fabulous violinist Dave Swarbrick. Then, something akin to a miracle happens. The spectators in the front rows start to hush up the talkers, and slowly the murmur of voices dies down. It seems that the young folk audience in London is ready to give this unknown, extremely shy, guitarist a chance.

"They listened in silence when he sang 'Three Hours'," Joe Boyd recalls, "then erupted in applause. Nick looked at them suspiciously, not sure how to smile.... Each song was rewarded with huge applause. I could feel the affection surging towards the stage. When he finished, the cheering soared and I pushed him back on the stage for an encore. As I stood watching from the wings, my mind was racing: *Nick can tour. He can play concerts after all. It doesn't matter that he can't talk to an audience. He'll learn how. He can have a real career. I'm not whistling in the dark, after all.*"

A neat middle-aged couple is sitting in one of the back rows.

"I'm sure we were the oldest people in the Hall that night," Molly says with a smile. "We almost had to sneak in, hoping that Nick wouldn't spot us."

"We were worried that he would get upset," Rodney explains.

"Afterwards we told him we had been there," Molly says.

"He was a tremendous success," Rodney emphasises.

"We were so very happy," Molly says. "Everyone was focused on the stage. We could see how the people around us were completely spellbound."

Rodney nods pensively, and adds after a little while: "But, John and Beverley Martin did a pretty good job, too. John is a real entertainer. He told jokes between songs…"

"But not Nick," Molly interjects.

"No, not Nick," Rodney agrees.

Molly: "In fact, he never spoke one word. He came on, wearing a jacket that was too short, his old black trousers, sat down and played six or seven songs; when he was done, he just got up and waved goodbye with his guitar and pushed off."

♪♪♪

Shortly after the Festival Hall concert the first real review of *Five Leaves Left* appears.

In the *New Musical Express* of 4 October, a critic with the initials G.C. writes about Nick Drake and The Fairport Convention: "They spent some time travelling together in Europe for some time, a trip which has greatly influenced his songwriting." And further: "His voice reminds me very much of Peter Sarstedt, but his songs lack Sarstedt's penetration and arresting quality." G.C. concludes: "There is not nearly enough variety on this debut LP to make it entertaining."

European tour? Peter Sarstedt? Entertaining?

Nick reads the review and is stunned. He is searching for one true word in there. Robert Kirby tries to cheer him up. And Joe Boyd, who is always busy, says that what he most looks forward to now is to go into the studio with Nick some time in the autumn. Because, of course they are going to make another album. No question about that.

"Focus on the songwriting," Boyd says. "Time is on your side. You'll have your breakthrough, just wait and see."

But whenever Nick stops at Island Records and asks how *Five Leaves Left* is doing, there is an awkward silence at the office. The fact is the album is just not selling. But so what? Chris Blackwell, the director, reassures Nick that sales of two to three thousand copies are quite normal for a debut artist. Days go by, become weeks and months, and there are no royalties. The songs are not getting any airplay on the radio. The record company has not released any singles from the album, and the question is whether that would have made any difference; it is hard to imagine that any of the ten songs would have entered the Top 40, which is dominated by hit acts such as Creedence Clearwater Revival, The Rolling Stones, and Elvis Presley.

After the disastrous review in *New Musical Express*, Nick goes on a tour of folk music clubs and pubs around Mid England. One day, he performs in the cafeteria of a Wolverhampton factory. The workers begin talking among themselves during the first song. During the next one they all begin clattering their plates and glasses, laughing and whistling, and when Nick ignores them, some bloke gets up and shouts: "Don't you know any songs we can sing along with?"

"Nick came home from Wolverhampton in relatively good spirits," Molly recalls. "He was laughing about the concert and said that it had all been one big joke. But, deep within, I think it really got to him. In his heart of hearts I think he was deeply hurt."

It is around this time – in November and December of 1969 – that Nick's mother notices something different about her boy. It is as if he is touchier about things. He can spend hours analysing trifles. Molly is astonished; she has never before seen her son like this. He starts referring to his record as a failure. Something is wrong with the sleeve, he explains. "Three Hours" is miscredited as "Sundown", the sequence of the songs on Side One is listed wrongly, and in the lyrics of "Fruit Tree", "stock" has become distorted into "stalk". "A tree with its stalk in the ground?" he says with a shake of his head: "People must take me for an idiot!"

Disappointment at low sales figures and lack of recognition?

Much later Molly is not sure. "If Nick had had a wild success with *Five Leaves Left* and people clamouring for him, I am not so sure that he would have stood the pressure of it and the emotional strain that follows on the heels of a success. On the other hand a success would probably have meant a lot to him."

One thing is worrying his parents. Nick often seems lethargic when he comes to visit at the weekends. His eyes are unclear, and sometimes he speaks slowly and strangely, even incoherently. He is smoking pot. And he does nothing to hide it. His father warns him. In India Rodney has seen how bad things can get when someone develops a dependency on marijuana: "You risk losing your ability to concentrate, losing it *for good.*" Nick thinks that Rodney is exaggerating. "All my friends at university smoke," he argues. "And you want me to quit. The thing is I am perfectly capable of controlling it."

While working on the songs for his next album he continues touring. He does the rounds of colleges and universities, folk music clubs and festivals, and in the course of the first six months of 1970 he gives more than twenty concerts.

On 21 February he performs at The Queen Elizabeth Hall, a smaller sister venue of The Royal Festival Hall. His friends John and Beverly Martyn are top of the bill. Nick is back in London. He had hoped to repeat the success of The Festival Hall, but on this occasion the audience is not as patient. As he is tuning his guitar between numbers people keep talking and some get up and go out for beer. He keeps fumbling with his capo, dropping it on the floor, sitting for a long time staring down at his shoes. David Sandison, the press secretary of Island Records, witnessed Nick's performance. "He left the stage with his shoulders hunched up, as if to protect himself from the embarrassment of even having to face people."

In March 1970 Nick is touring as the support act for Sandy Denny's new band, Fotheringay. After three concerts he phones Joe Boyd. "I can't take it any more," he says. "I'm coming home. I'm sorry."

After a few days' respite he goes back on the road. In May he plays together with his old idol Graham Bond, and later that month he is in the line-up for the Yorkshire Open Air

Festival, an event which attracts several thousand people. On 23 June we find him at the Ewell Technical College in Surrey along with folk musician Ralph McTell, known for the classic song "Streets of London".

"Nick sang beautifully that night, very hunched up, head down," McTell recalls. "About halfway through he just stopped, got up, and walked off the stage. I was puzzled because the audience was attentive, quiet, respectful, clapped in the right places. 'Is everything alright?' I asked. 'Oh, yeah,' he said. But it was clear that something upset him – or he had come to the conclusion that showbiz wasn't for him. The creative process was its own reward... although he could have been a great performer, because he had that sexy quietness and introspective 'marked-for-death' romantic poet look about him."

This was to be Nick's last concert.

In hindsight, music journalists and fans have criticised Joe Boyd for not hiring a band to back Nick up on tour. The least the American could have done for his solo artist was to make sure that a few helpers were there in the wings for Nick. His songs were complicated to perform live; he had to retune his guitar after almost every number, which distracted the audience. If he had had three or four guitars and a roadie to tune them, the whole thing might have turned out differently.

"It is correct that I was Nick's manager," Boyd confirms. "But I don't think we ever signed or negotiated a management deal. Such a thing requires that there is something to negotiate about. There was never any income, so the issue never arose."

Would it have helped Nick if he had had a band or some roadies to help during concerts?

Joe Boyd says no.

"When he decided to leave Cambridge and come to London and become a professional musician, the fact was that he wasn't able to match that step of going into the music business with going out and playing every night in a club, dealing with record companies, promotion and touring around," Boyd explains in a radio interview from 2007. It is the producer's impression that Nick tried to cocoon himself. "He isolated himself in a little bedsit in Hampstead, far from the rough and tumble of the rock scene. There was always a tension between those two sides of Nick: one part of him wanted to be a part of the world of commercial music; the other part revealed a shy, introverted person whose nature was not really cut out for standing on a stage, entertaining people. It was an elongated shock to Nick's system in terms of realising the difference between the world he had been in and the world he was now in and trying to compete in."

⁂

During this string of more or less successful concerts a letter appears from Françoise Hardy. It is addressed to Joe Boyd. The French *chanteuse* refers to *Five Leaves Left* in glowing terms, and wants to know if Nick Drake has the time and inclination to deliver some material for her forthcoming LP. Boyd is all fired up. He considers this offer a token of recognition for his young artist, and more than that: "Now we have a chance at reaching an international audience."

Through the sixties, Françoise Hardy was a regular guest on the French hit lists with her rather catchy, bittersweet ballads of love and youth; her records were released in Germany, Spain, and Italy. The English had also taken the tall, ravishing beauty to their hearts, especially after she had performed at the Savoy Hotel in London in 1965 and had started to be seen in the nightlife of Swinging London in the company of members of The Beatles and The Rolling Stones. There had been persistent rumours of collaborations between the world's two biggest rock bands and Françoise Hardy. It was also a well-known fact that Dylan had his eyes on her.[5] After a concert in Paris in the spring of 1966, he invited her to his hotel room and played two of his new, and as yet unrecorded, songs for her, "I Want You" and "Just Like a Woman". Despite good vibes, no actual collaboration was ever established.

In early June, Nick and Joe flew to Paris and visited Françoise Hardy in the artists' neighbourhood of the Île St. Louis, the island in the middle of the Seine, next to Montmartre.

It was a warm, sunny day. From Hardy's flat on the top floor there was a most glorious view of the Nôtre-Dame. But Nick spent the duration of the 45-minute meeting staring into his teacup. He, who spoke French quite well, left the hostess to try and express herself in broken English. He only gave monosyllabic answers to Hardy's questions about how they might collaborate.

"She seemed cheerful, very gracious and polite," Joe Boyd recalls. "Her assistant was there to help out so that we could settle the practicalities at once. But nothing came of it. I think she thought he was too strange."

---

5   On the back cover of *Another Side Of Bob Dylan* from 1964, Dylan printed a poem he had written for Françoise Hardy.

And perhaps Françoise Hardy forgot the young, gauche songwriter from England. *He*, however, did not forget her.

In October of 1974 Nick was staying on a barge on the Seine with some friends; from his cabin he had a view of the Île St. Louis.

After several years of exhausting bouts of depression, he had suddenly entered a good phase and – to the great joy of his family and friends – had hatched plans to record a new album. One day he looked up Françoise Hardy and asked if she was still interested in material. She was. "What are you doing in Paris?" she inquired. "At the moment I'm on holiday," he explained. "But I'm going to move over here. I'm looking for a flat. Next week I'm going back to England to pick up my things. You'll be hearing from me soon."

The Girl and the Monkey

Joey will come when once more it looks like snow
Joey will come when it's really time to go.

Until the start of the recording of *Five Leaves Left* in the summer of 1969 Nick has never had a regular girlfriend. He is good looking. He is charming. Girls have their eyes on that tall, slim fellow in the black coat and faded jeans when he shows up at parties at friends' houses with his guitar in hand.

His two schoolmates, Simon Crocker and Jeremy Mason, both believe he was a very gentle and chivalrous man whenever he had dealings with the fairer sex.

"Nick was not a big predator," Jeremy Mason explains. "But if there happened to be a lot of girls around, he quite liked to play it a little mysterious. That actually is one way of attracting them to you. I'm sure he enjoyed the interest that sparked – even if he didn't always follow up on it."

Simon Crocker: "Most of the women we met in Aix-en-Provence were older than us. We were English public schoolboys, novices in terms of sexual experience, probably terribly immature and awkward. On top of that, none of us spoke French very well. But I have a very clear memory of Nick running off with one vicar's daughter. She was blonde – and English."

"My girlfriend fancied him enormously," Robert Kirby recalls. "Many of the girls I knew back then were attracted to Nick. And, yes, he was very shy – his bashfulness when confronted with the opposite sex has led to all these speculations as to whether he really was gay, a closet homosexual, of course."

The arranger scratches his beard and hesitates for a moment. "The thing is that those who make a lot out of this issue have entirely the wrong idea. They think that Cambridge was still a part of Victorian England in the sixties. *Excuse me!* I had loads of gay friends at university. Several of my professors and tutors were gay and no one as much as lifted an eyebrow on that account. I'm willing to claim that it was more acceptable to be gay at the end of the sixties than it is today. Remember sexual liberation was very much a part of our political agenda. Now, as it happens, Nick was *not* gay. Had he been, I would of course have known about it. I mean, we spent a great deal of our youth together; we often saw each other three or four times a week. When we lived in Cambridge he would go to London in the weekends and I know that he spent the night with various women. I know that he had affairs. He just didn't go round shouting about it."

⁂

Rodney and Molly had several experiences of their son falling in love with someone, but it was as if he had a way of opposing the girls who were interested in him, as if he rapidly felt misunderstood and rejected; however slender the basis for those feelings might seem to his parents. On the other hand, if Nick became really close to a girl, he did not let go of her. Certainly, several of his affairs developed into friendships. And there was the case of the beautiful and sensitive Sophia Ryde whom he had met in the musicians' circles in London and often visited during the recording of *Five Leaves Left*. He invited Sophia to the Isle of Wight Festival, the summer when Bob Dylan was the headliner. But Nick never heard his hero play. He sat all night long playing his own guitar in the small tent he had borrowed from a friend from university.

"Sophia Ryde was a frequent topic of discussion in our house," Rodney smiles. "I think he was quite keen on her. But we only met her at the funeral. Sweet girl. We exchanged letters with her after Nick's death"

Another of Nick's London affairs, Daisy Burlison-Rush, was a girl he kept in touch with throughout the last five years of his life. During those periods when he was incapable of working because of depression, he would come to Daisy's apartment and sit for hours and stare into thin air.

"Women like Sophia and Daisy learned how to handle Nick when he was having a hard time," Molly says. "One time he left here in a very bad state and was not heard from for weeks. We had no idea where he was and we were getting more and more worried. Then one day the doorbell rang and there was Daisy with Nick. He was so bad that he couldn't even speak. He just shrugged and disappeared into his room. 'I'm sorry,' Daisy said, 'but I thought I ought to bring him home. If I had phoned you he would probably just have left.'"

"His skin was white and transparent – you could almost see right through him," Linda Thompson recalls. The Scottish singer – then Linda Peters before her marriage to Richard Thompson from Fairport Convention – met Nick through Joe Boyd and the circle of artists the producer had established through Witchseason. It was in the spring of 1970; Nick was twenty-one, Linda twenty-two. They would meet in her Notting Hill flat where they would sit and drink Mu tea and listen to records, mostly blues, Thompson remembers. "If I put on some things of the day, he would go up to the record player and, wordlessly, just take it off. He would often stay overnight, and then, the following morning I'd go across the street with him and give him a ten-shilling note to get home, because he never had any money."

♪♪♪

Rain's the way you move now, Nick sings in one of those compositions he discarded during the recording of his first album, perhaps because he felt that the melody was too close to one of Donovan's standard, C-major songs. The lyrics are about a failed relationship. In dense images we hear of a love that cannot cope with everyday routines:

> *This was our season and we said it couldn't end*
> *But my love left with the rain.*

It is as if Nick at an early age lands in a chronic state of unhappy love. He feels let down by girls, by friends, by the world as such. And he feels that he lets himself down. And when – for reasons lost in an inner darkness – one cannot simply reach out and pick the ripe fruits of life and mature in accordance with the guidelines laid out by life, what then? Nick responds by building up a world of his own, an idyllic universe populated by princesses; fair supernatural creatures who he dreams will descend from heavenly palaces and free him from his loneliness. "Princess of the

Sand," he calls one of his saving angels with a touch of gallows humour. Even she fails him in the decisive moment: *She moved her mouth but there came no sound/The message she brought can never be found...*

Nick has long since given up addressing his great love. No one can know what she thinks. No one can know why she suddenly turns her back or walks out in the rain, why she smiles or why she sighs, where she's been or whom she's seen. No one can know, especially not her lover who sings to her. So why not call her the "princess of the sky" and say that she is on a journey to the stars? Away from earth. Away from Nick. And yet her name is Mary Jane, and she has brightly coloured eyes.

He likes the name Jane. It's good to sing: two soft consonants and one long vowel to create a musical phrase from.

In "Hazey Jane I" Nick shows a side of his poetry where he does *not* put the loved one on a pedestal, but addresses her directly. The stanzas are built up as a series of questions, and in their possible answers he draws an image of himself and his own situation:

> *Do you feel like a remnant*
> *Of something that's past?*
> *Do you find things are moving*
> *Just a little too fast?*

Almost all of his love songs are about being left behind. Feeling abandoned is one of the core symptoms of depression, but at the same time extremely conducive to the creative process of the depressed artist. Perhaps Nick, deep down, wishes to be abandoned. Perhaps that is the way in which he uses love: as the blues, as a state of mind, as fuel for his songs and through that as a means to create his unique world of beauty. It is the poetry and the melodies that keep him going, the songs become his lifeline to the world, the way in which he communicates. Or as he puts it in "Hazey Jane II":

If songs were lines in a conversation
The situation would be fine.

♪♪♪

In the autumn of 1969 Nick often frequents London. He is about to start his next offering and the Sound Techniques Studio is in Old Church Street, Chelsea. A mile away – on the other side of the Thames – is Battersea, where his sister Gabrielle lives. Nick gets to use a room there; an ideal arrangement which means that he is close to the studio and can come and go exactly as he pleases. He puts his things into storage, leaves Cambridge, and moves in with his sister. But after a few weeks he informs Gabrielle that he is moving in with a girlfriend. Who she is, what her name is, and where he has met her he doesn't say.

This girl has a flat in Notting Hill Gate. And a monkey, which on closer inspection turns out to be a Guenon; an agile little fellow with a long tail and a curious pair of eyes. The monkey leaps around the rooms, swinging like Tarzan from curtains and lamps, shits on the floor, screams and makes a fuss, and often sits in the window grooming itself.

The friends who come and see Nick in the flat cannot quite figure out the relationship between him and the girl. Are they lovers? Bedfellows? Or are they just keeping each other company and conveniently sharing the flat?

"She was a bit of a hippie," explains Brian Wells, one of Nick's friends from Cambridge who had moved to London to study medicine. "She hardly ever spoke. She would usually sit in a corner and stitch little cushions for Nick; don't ask me what she thought he would do with them."

"She was never there when I came to see him," says Robert Kirby. "We would usually smoke a joint. 'What would you like to listen to?' Nick would ask. 'Put on the monkey,' I would say. He didn't need any goading, because as soon as the turntable would start spinning the animal would jump on top of it. Then we would sit and watch the monkey go round and round. That was one of our great pleasures. And the monkey liked it."

In October Nick drops out of university. Now he is going to devote himself completely to his songwriting he explains to his friends, and to his puzzled parents who only object feebly.

He leaves the girl's flat and never mentions her again. She disappears from his life like the princesses he keeps singing of. But this princess was made of flesh and blood; she just wasn't the answer to his dreams, not a fairy tale princess.

He takes a room in Belsize Park, Hampstead. Here he walls himself in for the winter, intent on creating an album that has to be even more fulfilling than *Five Leaves Left*.

Bryter Layter

London is grey and overcast, fog and drizzle from morning to night. Rain, day and night, on the city windows. Down the glass facades. Down the walls. Down onto the greasy asphalt roads. And into the gutters and down the sewers.

Taxis are passing, neon signs flashing, river barges tooting. And the hours are flowing. Day slips into night and night slips into day, and the distinction between the two is slowly erased. Only the clocks tell time. And the clocks are ticking, the windscreen wipers clicking, and the city bells chiming in the damp air. Late November.

Nick is sitting in his flat on Haverstock Hill in Hampstead, his guitar on his lap, tuning the strings, half listening to the crackle of a transistor radio in the background. The storm warnings. The shipping news. Far away a voice declaring that the weather will be brighter later.

Later he leaves his room. He goes out in the traffic, among the pigeons and the crowds of pedestrians teeming through the city, escaping down escalators, into tube stations, department stores, and office buildings. On stairs, in lifts in tall, slim buildings, and long underground corridors: businessmen, messengers, civil servants, and tourists going up and down and back and forth. Crisscrossing, in all directions, on separate floors in the big city cubes.

Later, he turns his back on the crowds and disappears into Regent's Park. With long, loping strides, his elbows held close to his body, he moves through the deserted gardens, working his way along winding paths up to Primrose Hill where the trees stand on the slope, leaning into winter, naked, crippled with age. When he gets to the top he turns around to gaze at the flickering cones of light down on Prince Albert Road. On the horizon, the endless city looms like a giant electrical relay. And everywhere between Primrose Hill and the southern night sky lies London, shrouded in fog and neon. London on a November night: a pin cushion of lights, shimmering and flickering in the dusk.

He lights a joint, bends down to tie his shoelaces, without quite being able to tell whether he is awake or in the middle of a dream, whether what he sees is a real city or a scenario from a science fiction film without a title, without a director.

Later Nick is standing on the side of one of the innumerable approach roads circling the city. Leaning back, dressed in black, with his elbows resting on a rail protruding from an underground stairway. Behind the road the moon comes up, round and yellow like an old brass coin, and between Nick and the moon hovers a car, bathed in the bluish lights of a row of neon lamps from above. A car in the city space, on its way, as in a flash it separates Nick from eternity behind the guard rail.

He is waiting for dawn, waiting for the rising sun to clear the sky of clouds, the city sky as well as his own inner northern sky. And all day long he is working his way around the streets and the squares, waiting for the night, just to stand there on the outskirts of an abandoned neighbourhood, looking for the moon.

He is waiting for a diffuse, never realised "later." A bright spell in the evening, the "brighter later" the meteorologist promised. Nick steals those two words for a song about his own meteorology and that of the city some days in November, and later he picks that song as the title for his new album. He spells "brighter later" differently, in a more mysterious, more poetic way, much as one would imagine Shakespeare might have done, or a stoned person with a sense of humour. "Brighter Later" becomes the cryptic *Bryter Layter*, but it still refers to a form of weather report. Look up at the sky, get a fix on the clouds, and off you go. Out into the city squares and back home again.

And what will happen in the morning when the world
    it gets
So crowded that you can't look out the window in the
    morning.

Nick opens the curtains and looks out in a daze at the world racing by outside his window. The world is waiting, the world demands that you take part in the ever-growing race back and forth, up and down the stairs, in and out the door. Ask no questions, lift your feet off the ground, weigh up your anchor, and for God's sake never look back.

And what will happen when you come home?

Turn around and come back again.

That is the opening of "Hazey Jane II". Trumpets and electric guitar, up front. In the middle of the big city bustle. Nick is a stranger in the streets. He is watching the faces, in the mirrors, behind car windows, on the double-decker buses shuttling across the city; he is listening to the clanking of typewriters, hurried conversations across tables, on telephones and at ticket hatches, small talk streaming out from open doors and windows:

For the sound of a busy place
Is fine for a pretty face
Who knows what a face is for?

"Bryter Layter" is a song of the city, urban jazz, urban dance. An instrumental soundtrack for an unmade film, enraptured blue ballads reflecting the mental vacuum of the tobacconist after closing time. The band is augmented with a saxophone while drums and percussion feature prominently in the mix. On a couple of songs John Cale, the Welsh wizard who long ago left the avant-garde Velvet Underground, plays along. Cale bows his electric viola and coaxes a double timbre from his instrument. He also plays the celeste and the organ to deepen the dark side of *Bryter Layter*. It does have a dark side, for the album reflects shadow and light, the rhythm of day and night is mirrored in the changes between inner and outer worlds; between dark visions and open poetry, as clear as day. Big city poetry, the melody of the day, the quickstep of feet across a city square. A track that captures the pulse of London, "At the Chime of a City Clock" is inspired by the numerous bells of London's many churches. Listen to the rhythm of the melody, fast syncopated pulses, underscored by Ray Warleigh's fluttering trills on the sax, and listen to the lyrics, a little masterpiece of musical language:

Stay indoors beneath the floors
Talk with neighbours only
The games you play make people say
You're either weird or lonely.

"Poor Boy" is another song where Nick captures the specific feeling of unrest and disquiet, which draws loners and outsiders to street corners and doorways in the heart of the city and in surrounding, nameless, squalid quarters. The enticing bossa nova rhythm of the guitar, a chorus of gospel girls, and the tingling jazz riffs of South African pianist Chris McGregor all contribute to bring out the singer's London spleen, as Nick mockingly spins his loathing for life out in long playful chains of rhyme, throwing the words up in the air, over his shoulder like destiny's coin-toss, ironic towards his own pretentiousness:

I'm a poor boy
And I'm a ranger
Things I say
May seem stranger
Than Sunday
Changing to Monday.

It's not just what Nick says that can seem strange. The jottings he occasionally puts down in his notebook also seem odd. Oddly out of touch with the world, to put it mildly.

He is thinking in fragments; lets himself be guided by sudden absurd fancies. And he is always philosophising about what business he has being in this body that so happens to bear the name of Nick Drake. Sure, he can pinch himself and feel the pain and thereby reassure himself that he is real, that he exists as a being made of flesh and blood. But behind all the grimaces, behind the shelter of his skin, and way into his bones, behind the throbbing of his pulse he feels that he is empty. Dead. A thing.

I could have been a signpost, could have been a clock/As

simple as a kettle, steady as a rock, he sings quietly in "One of These Things First", as the piano in the background does a carefree climb up and down the minor scale. There is no cause for panic. The poet is just making the point to himself that he is not here, that this fragile *I* he has been carrying around has now gone up in smoke. Gone with the wind. What is left fades away into a diffuse *could have been*.

So many chances of a life, even a non-life, wasted opportunities, vainly striving for anything, and now life itself is lost for life; the sudden, vital possibility of physical presence.

I could be even here/I would be, I should be so near.

The astonishing thing about this song is actually that Nick feels so close. In the middle of his absence he is able to create a great intensity; a tension between tones and words into which the listener can step, and be. The door is open, you can walk right in, there is plenty of space within the music, and the message of the lyrics is written between the lines. The singer is seeking his own way with his voice, with his inscrutable words. He seeks but finds nothing. And yet he finds a way through time and space and reaches you *here and now*. Listen for yourself.

> *I never felt magic crazy as this*
> *I never saw moons knew the meaning of the sea*
> *I never held emotion in the palm of my hand*
> *Or felt sweet breezes in the top of a tree*
> *But now you're here*
> *Brighten my northern sky.*

All at once the bell jar that surrounds Nick bursts open. And the darkness is shot through with light and clear visions. "Northern Sky" is a clear and mysterious song. Arthur Lubow calls this special kind of beauty which Nick conjures up "the magic of innocence." But "Northern Sky" is more than that. And while this penultimate track on the album is named "the greatest love song of modern times" thirty years after the fact by *New Musical Express*, "Northern Sky" is much more than just a three-chord love song. Here we are dealing with a mystical rebirth, a person who finds himself, and in one fleeting moment reaches his hand up into a vast receding space. He transcends himself, sensing acutely – he is present as never before. He moves and is moved by forces stemming from a higher world.

I never felt magic crazy as this…

In a moment the ecstasy is over.

In a moment this marvellous connection will break.

John Cale throws light on Nick's vision. With an accompaniment that is pure magic and devotion, he escorts his vocalist to the peak of his performance. Plays his piano, strikes his chimes. With purity.

They are two buttoned-up souls meeting. Their point of contact is in the music. That is where the connection is made. That is where it is fulfilled. And out streams a previously unheard serenade, a moonbeam of tones.

▲▮▮

The process of recording *Bryter Layter* is a drawn-out affair. Nick, ever the perfectionist, cannot reach agreement with Joe Boyd on which tracks to include on the album. In the middle of the recording sessions he discards "Things Behind the Sun", a song he wrote in the autumn of 1969 when he moved from Cambridge to London. Joe thinks that is one of Nick's best songs ever. On the other hand the producer is not fond of the four instrumental pieces Nick has composed. Joe wants to make a classic singer-song-writer album. Nick wants to make a concept album. Each side has to open and close with an instrumental track, he explains. The lyrics of the seven other songs must reflect and elaborate on each other, induce a certain state, a certain atmosphere; the melodies slip from one to the next without the listener noticing, sending echoes into each other, so that in one song you hear the whole album, and in the whole album you hear the same song – like a chime of Sunday morning bells.

This discussion leads to a compromise. Out goes "Things Behind the Sun". So does one of the instrumentals, and thus part of the concept. Nick objects in his own quiet manner. He becomes stubborn and contrary, several times walking out of the studio over trifles. He really *does* hate compromises.

But Joe Boyd is thoroughly convinced that *Bryter Layter* will become Nick Drake's breakthrough. That is why he spends every available hour – in between his eleven other productions that year – on working with the tracks, calling in new musicians and experimenting with the sound and the arrangements. The album is remixed several times, including at the Vanguard Studio in New York.

The final result must have excited Boyd because when he is subsequently asked to enumerate his merits as a producer, he singles out *Bryter Layter* as his most complete work. He refers to Nick's record as a masterpiece.

But Nick's masterpiece does not sell.

At the two trendsetting English music magazines, *Melody Maker* and *New Musical Express*, they are busy writing about Johnny Cash and Frank Sinatra. They don't trouble themselves reviewing a singer who does nothing to promote himself. There are no receptions with free beer and free records. No interviews. There are no concert plans either. Immediately after the record is released in November, Nick picks up his guitar, leaves the music scene, and isolates himself in his flat on Haverstock Hill. He would like to start writing new songs but lacks the energy. Everyone around is raving about *Bryter Layter*, telling him that he has made a fantastic record, just like they did when *Five Leaves Left* came out. He needs a break to think. Was it worth all the hard work? This whole circus he's been living over the past fourteen months – was he selling his soul in this constant chase after fame and fortune?

And it's back to winter again, and nothing has changed.

Nick puts rugs in his window sills, wraps himself in sweaters to keep warm, wears his long, black woollen coat inside the apartment. There are days when he can't play guitar, days when he stays under the covers even when there is a knock on the door.

The landlord has shut off the gas because the lodger on the ground floor has not paid his bills.

♪♪♪

On 1 January 1971, Joe Boyd sells his production company to Chris Blackwell, founder of Island Records. Shortly after that, the American goes back to the States to begin his new job as director of music for Warner Bros, Los Angeles. For Nick, Boyd's departure comes as a shock. He hasn't been told. Suddenly his mentor and protector has gone; despite their differences this was a man who shared his musical vision – a professional from the industry who also happened to have become a close friend. Why is Joe leaving him in the lurch now when he needs his friend's support more than ever?

That question just barely crosses his troubled mind before it becomes a new calamity, to add to the long list of misfortunes that have been dogging him. And it is no comfort that Boyd calls from across the Atlantic to reassure Nick that he will be fine without him. Joe explains that he has had a clause written into Nick's contract that his records must never be deleted from the Island back catalogue without consulting him first. He needn't have bothered: Chris Blackwell loves *Five Leaves Left* and *Bryter Layter* and even considers Nick Drake to be England's greatest acoustic guitarist…

A troubled cure for a troubled mind – that is exactly the way he himself had summed it up once. But what if the cure doesn't work? He shuts himself off from the world. Or is it really the world that shuts him off? Why aren't his records selling? And why has he never been able to find the girl he has dreamed of so intensely, the *princess of the sand*?

Nick withdraws once more. And survives on the cheque for 15 quid that the record company sends him once a week as a tacit acknowledgement of his talent. He still has not received a single penny in royalties.

⫶

"After *Bryter Layter* it went downhill quickly for Nick," poet and folk musician Paul Wheeler says. This former university friend from Cambridge had moved to Ascot, west of

London, and Nick sometimes dropped by. "I recall that he once said that he felt like a novice at being depressed. Nick had never imagined that he could find himself in a desperate situation. He was shaken to the core. He kept complaining that everything was slipping through his hands. He felt that he was guided from above – this guidance working through the record company, the producers, and the general system. He was losing control over his life. And it came as a complete surprise to him."

"The funny thing about *Bryter Layter* is that it's quite a happy album," Robert Kirby claims. "There is no doubt that Nick wrote those songs during a period when he was in crisis. He was living in this large, high-ceilinged room on Haverstock Hill. There was a mattress on the floor. Next to the mattress was his guitar in a black case. That's all the décor I remember. A mattress and a guitar."

In the spring of 1971 Nick gives up the lease and moves to a smaller and cheaper room in Muswell Hill, a couple of miles north of Hampstead. He doesn't leave a forwarding address with the record company or any of his friends. To his parents he says that he wants peace and quiet to compose.

"I lived nearby," Robert Kirby recounts. "He would come by a couple of times a week, sit in a corner and stare into space. He didn't eat. He looked dishevelled. His clothes were dirty, his hair shaggy, his nails black with grime. His new room was horrible. I mean, Haverstock Hill was bohemian. But the room on Muswell Hill Road looked like a tomb. Not that it was seedy. It just had no life in it at all."

"One day he took out his guitar and played me a song. I listened, not knowing that that would be the last thing he would ever play for me. The funny thing is that a few years prior I had recorded that exact song as Nick was writing it. I still have that tape: a half hour where he is jamming his way towards 'Things Behind the Sun'."

⚏

One night in October the phone rings at Sound Techniques, the studio which is located in an abandoned workshop in the middle of Chelsea, London's old artist quarter. John Wood, the sound engineer, is busy at the mixer. He answers the phone. It's Nick. He wants to know if Wood has some time. "For what?" Wood asks, surprised. "My new record," Nick says. "I'm ready." "Excellent," Wood says, all of a sudden remembering the date they set up a few weeks ago. They had agreed to get together as soon as Nick had his new material together. "But what about production?" Wood had said. "Joe Boyd is in America, you know." "Exactly," Nick had replied. "The next album will be without Joe. Next time we do it my way."

Now the songs are there. John Wood knows that if he waits too long they might not be there anymore. He also knows that Chris Blackwell is very interested in a new Nick Drake record. Therefore the engineer takes out his calendar and starts looking for an opening in his jammed schedule. He only has availability after eleven o'clock at night.

A few nights later, Nick arrives with his guitar.

John Wood begins to set up his gear. He places a chair in the middle of the elongated, high-ceilinged room with the unfinished walls, and begins to set up a number of microphones. That doesn't take very long.

Nick explains to Wood that he wants the guitar and vocals recorded at the same time, just as they have always done. Then he gets into the recording room and begins to play. After each song he retunes his guitar and moves the capo up or down the fret board all according to the key. The guitar rings out loud; Nick's voice is almost painfully intense in the large space.

The next evening he meets up with Wood again and they pick up where they left off. They do a second take of some of the songs and Nick adds piano to one track; plays a small bell-like solo on the Steinway grand piano which Wood had bought for the studio years back with his own savings.

"Afterwards, when we sat in the control room and listened to the tapes, I asked Nick how much of the material he thought we should keep," John Wood recollects. "'All of it,' Nick replied. I was surprised; we had never worked like that before. I realised that he had no more songs. It would be a short album – and an unusually intense one. 'How would you like to have the songs arranged?' I asked. 'I don't want them arranged,' Nick said. 'I want them to stand naked. No frills!'"

Pink Moon

Saw it written and I saw it say
Pink moon is on its way
And none of you stand so tall
Pink moon gonna get ye all
It's a pink, pink, pink, pink, pink moon.

Nick sees the writing on the water: the moon is on its way, the round lifeless moon. Slowly rising on the horizon, only to mirror its silver in the cove. An evening in August where the mist is rising from the ground and the insects are restlessly buzzing.

Do you also see a symbol written in the middle of the black water? Do not interpret it; there is nothing to interpret. Your sudden disquiet is answered by a faint hiss from space. That is the sound of the moon. There is nothing to grasp. Only this is apparent: that the moon is approaching with its white light. And its almost inaudible hiss.

Look up towards the sun on a clear summer's day, and then let your gaze glide across the landscape. You see blades of grass, trees and flowers sucking in light. On the night of the full moon you see only the pale reflection of the sun. You see a blind eye on high. You see the eye of night whose iris spreads like phosphorous rings in the dark.

Walk out into sleepless space.
Walk out into shadeless blue.

Over the water's bright mirror: mosquito columns and thin drifting clouds. August is raining down from the stars.

The moon is on its way.

⁂

The songs are complex in their structure, and at the same time as simple as haiku poems: despite the fragility and pain that Nick puts on display, they are far from unequivocally dark. There is a resigned calm present on *Pink Moon*, such as is found in someone who has settled his account and is ready to face the consequences of an important choice. He has given up on love but not on life. Several of the short songs on the album seem to be written to the woman who has failed him:

> *And I was green, greener than the hill*
> *Where flowers grew and the sun shone still*
> *Now I'm darker than the deepest sea*
> *Just hand me down, give me a place to be*
> …
> *Now I'm weaker than the palest blue*
> *Oh, so weak in this need for you.*

Nick transforms this loss of love into beauty. The melancholia of the words is made luminous by his voice, by the guitar; as long as the music plays, the harmony is in a certain way redressed, even though he is powerless to win back his beloved.

In his early, unpublished songs and on *Five Leaves Left* Nick succeeds in reconstructing elements of a lost paradise, akin to the land of childhood, a universe of oblivion and magic; of an innocence that can be traced back to the first stage of falling in love. On *Pink Moon* he has left all this behind; he is older and more disillusioned. But he holds on to the poetry, holds on to the metaphysics as a way of perceiving reality, and he refuses to surrender to silence. He is performing a work of mourning; a necessary labour where each note, each word, is balancing on a knife's edge.

Two songs stand out, not just because of their length. Nick wrote "Parasite" and "Things Behind the Sun" in 1969, when he was living in Cambridge. The latter was created in the clouds of marijuana in Robert Kirby's college room. While the guitar insists on repeating the same riff, Nick piles rhyme upon rhyme, giving his imagination free rein, until the lines *And the movement in your brain/Sends you out into the rain* close the song – like a sudden bombshell striking a fragile mind. This is an accurate portrait of a melancholic. Forces he could not master, a whim, a signal from his unconscious sent him outside the community – self-destructive, inexplicable. But sometimes strangely liberating.

Nick loves the word "rain." It recurs in many of his songs and the metaphor has a double ring. On the one hand it symbolises an exclusion from the community, the person left standing alone in the rain. The more it pours, the more acutely is the state of being abandoned elaborated and enforced (this allegory is used in blues and soul, but not often in rock music). On the other hand, the allegory is most often positively charged in Nick's universe; rain for him means catharsis. That goes for all of his early compositions, and not least for his key song "River Man":

For when she thought of summer rain
Calling for her mind again
She lost the pain
And stayed for more.

In "Mickey's Tune" a connection is made between rain and the lost land of childhood; here, what comes pouring down is a warm rainfall, with associations of the monsoon which was a phenomenon Nick experienced in his early childhood. The rainy season in Burma begins in May and ends in October. Hiding behind the metaphor there is a longing for a deeper harmony, possibly a longing to be back in the safe waters of the womb; perhaps he is healing the separation from his very earliest love object with these rain songs.

In the circular movement from death to birth on *Pink Moon* lies at least one of the answers as to why the album is not perceived as depressing. The artist is able to transcend painful emotions such as sorrow and melancholia. He ends up declaring his love to the rhythm of day and night, to the cycle of nature, to life itself – in "From the Morning":

And now we rise
And we are everywhere.

⁂

Shortly after Nick has handed over the master tape to Chris Blackwell at Island Records and cashed a cheque for five hundred pounds to cover the studio expenses, he moves from Muswell Hill to Tanworth-in-Arden. This is

November 1971. He needs to recuperate after a period of violent mood swings and sleepless nights.

"He came home with plans to start a new album," Rodney recalls. "'I've got music running through my head all the time,' he told me. But he never touched his guitar. He didn't do anything, except drive his car around. Often he wanted to go to London. He would leave after lunch and a couple of hours later the phone would ring: 'I've run out of petrol. Can you come and fetch me?'"

"We used to set off all over the country rescuing Nick," Molly laughs. "He would get stranded in all sorts of places, Oxford, Yorkshire, Eastbourne..."

Rodney: "I thought we were the only ones he didn't want to talk to, until I realised that he had no contact with even his closest friends. We invited John Martyn to come up one weekend, to cheer him up. John is an energetic extrovert and very direct in his ways. Nick went to bed early, Molly and I stayed up. We sat here in the living room and chatted with John until two in the morning. He said: 'Whenever you leave Nick, you always feel that you let him down.' And that is absolutely true. You always felt that you were letting Nick down. You had this constant guilt. And you would wonder what you had said or done that was somehow wrong."

Molly: "We managed to have him admitted to St. Thomas' Hospital in London. He was in the psychiatric ward for a month. We were lucky enough to get in touch with one of the best psychiatrists in the country, a man who was famous for his results with depressive patients – a real authority in his field." She hesitates a bit: "Something went wrong between the psychiatrist and us. It never really worked out, and when it comes down to it: what do psychiatrists really know about the human mind? Not much, I'm afraid. They are still terribly in the dark."

Nick leaves St. Thomas' with a prescription for three different drugs: an anti-depressant, an anti-psychotic, and a drug for convulsions. It's something with his brain chemistry, the doctor has told him. Something with adjusting balances. His diagnosis is endogenous depression.[6]

"We had to persuade him to take his medication." Rodney sits up straight on the sofa, stares ahead lost in thought, biting his lower lip. "The anti-depressants helped him, I have no doubts about that. Nick was gradually getting better: one could see that. The thing was that he hated the medicine. He hated going to the psychiatrist. Sometimes he would take all his pills and pour them down the drain."

⌁

Pink Moon is released on 25 February 1972. Apart from press secretary David Sandison's very personal, full-page ad in the widely circulated English music magazines the month before, the release is utterly without fanfare. One of the few places where the record is reviewed is *Melody Maker*. Here, critic Mark Plummer writes on 1 May: "Drake is a fairly mysterious person, no-one appears to know where he lives, what he does – apart from writing songs – and there is not even a chance of seeing him on stage to get closer to his insides…. Perhaps one should

---

6   A depression that comes from within, and is not rooted in external
    circumstances. Endogenous depression corresponds roughly to what
    was previously known as "melancholia".

play his albums with the sound off and just look at the cover and make the music in your head reciting his words from inside the cover to your own rhythmic heart rhymes. Nick Drake does not exist at all."

The reviewer is closer to the truth than he knows on this last point. When the envelope containing the clipping from *Melody Maker* arrives at Far Leys, Nick is in his deepest crisis. He doesn't eat, he doesn't change his clothes, and he can't even be bothered to listen to music. He is a shadow in a dark room. There is no Saturday sun, no Sunday rain here, the singer has put his guitar in a case and drawn the curtains. He does not set foot outdoors, but he doesn't want to remain where he is either. It's been like that for several weeks now, and neither his sister Gabrielle nor his parents can persuade him to be admitted to St. Thomas' again.

Rodney: "He said that he hated life. That he could see no point in going on. Life was empty and meaningless. That sort of talk made me so terribly worried. I didn't know what to tell him; and if I had known he would hardly have listened."

"The longest period where he was out of treatment was six months," Molly recalls. "'I intend to go through this in my own way,' he said to me one night when we were sitting in the kitchen. 'The problem is that I have failed at everything I've done. How could some London doctor make up for a lifetime of mistakes?'"

From the music room one can sometimes hear the faint notes of violins and trumpets. It is one of Bach's

Brandenburg Concertos spinning on the gramophone. But Nick has turned down the volume, so that the music is on the brink of silence. When the record is finished he lets the cartridge continue in the inner groove.

Nick listens to the faint noise of the needle for hours on end.

And the hours pass; day turns to night.

In the corner room on the first floor the light is off. There is a silhouette in the dark. It's Nick in the lotus position on his bed, looking at the cream painted walls. He sits motionless like a Buddha. Only a nocturnal moth fluttering against the ceiling manages for an instant to interfere with the circles of his silence – with its monotonous hum, its transparent wings. When the round window facing the garden becomes tinted red, he has climbed under his bedspread. He is fully dressed with his legs curled up under him; he does not reply when his mother knocks on the door.

One weekend he visits John and Sheila Wood in Suffolk – only to sit in a corner of their garden, watching Wood's two daughters play catch on the lawn. When Sheila Wood comes out with a tray of tea and biscuits, he is gone as suddenly as he appeared.

Another weekend he drives down to John and Beverly Martyn's house in Hastings, the fishing village with the tall, black, wooden towers, one of England's magical places where a few years earlier he had written "Northern Sky". He spends two days staring across the sea at the fishing boats sailing by, their course set for harbour or the blue horizon.

One day Nick says he wants to be an ordinary person with an ordinary job and asks his father to help him.

Despite his own misgivings Rodney manages to get him a job with a computer firm, which have a training scheme in London. Nick begins on a Monday morning at nine. At four o'clock the company boss looks around for his new employee, in vain. Later he learns that the young man had disappeared out the back door.

⫛

The days go like that. Nick wakes up with a hangover, but he hasn't been drinking. He gets on his feet, but most of all he feels like staying in bed, pulling the covers over his head, and sleeping it all off. But he cannot sleep. He eats, but he does not enjoy the food. He gets in his car, goes out on the road, changes his mind, and turns back. He smokes cigarettes, watches TV, and listens to records, keeps up the routines.

He is caught in a trap, forced to choose between two evils. As long as he swallows his daily dose of psychotropic drugs, he can more or less keep the depression at bay. But the medicine dulls him and makes him lethargic. He cannot live without writing songs. He cannot write songs when he is medicated. When he drops the pills and starts to compose, the depression returns, stronger each time. Those periods when he isolates himself from the surrounding world get longer and longer. That is how the days pass, how they disappear like leaves in a calendar. All the pages are blank.

Hanging on a Star

One night in March 1974 Nick calls John Wood to tell him that he has some new songs ready. Shortly after, they meet up at the studio and begin recording the fourth Nick Drake album. It is rapidly clear, however, that the artist is not happy with his material. The lyrics are not working. There are several songs that are missing a chorus, or a stanza or two. Nick explains that he has run out of words. John Wood labels the tapes with dates and titles, and files them away in his office. These are raw demos, not master tapes.

In July Joe Boyd comes to London on summer vacation. When he sees how poorly Nick is and hears of the failed record project, he proposes that they give it a second chance along with Wood. The trio meet up in the studio late at night and begin to re-record the songs. But Nick has a problem playing guitar and singing the vocals at the same time; his voice breaks when he hits the high notes and he has a hard time remembering the lyrics. He ends up leaving the studio. Joe Boyd brings him back and persuades him to try again.

When Nick listens to the recordings at home he decides to put an end to his songwriting. He tells his parents that he has decided to quit and that this is a final decision.

"What about your new songs?" Molly asks.

"No good."

"Is that what they say at Island?"

"No."

"And what does Joe Boyd say?"

"Joe says they are OK."

"Then what is the problem?" Molly says

"The problem is," Nick says, "that the songs are not working at all. I cannot vouch for them, Mum. They are substandard."

Much later, when his parents hear four of the five songs, they have to agree with their son. "Normally, Nick would spend a long time writing a song," Rodney explains. "As far as I could see, part of the method was to wait. He would make a draft, put it away – often for months – pick it up again, tirelessly pursue it until every note sounded exactly the way he wanted it to. Those last songs, on the other hand, were written in a short time – in a period when he was extremely restless. If he had had a chance to re-record the songs, they would probably have become better."

"Yes, much better," Molly confirms. She hesitates. "Only, the thing was that the world had heard nothing from Nick for more than two years. He felt that something had to happen. And then this article appeared in *ZigZag*, 'In Search of Nick Drake', written by a chap called Connor McKnight. After two years of silence someone was saying that he wasn't forgotten. That meant a tremendous amount to him."

After having dropped the medicine over the summer, Nick is back on the anti-depressants.

Rodney: "He was worse than ever when one of his friends popped up; a teacher from Cambridge who had given him extra coaching in maths once when he was considering changing his study programme. This fellow was much older than Nick and not musical at all. He in fact seemed like the diametric opposite of our boy, mentally strong and an extrovert. When this man saw how bad things were he decided to take matters into his own hands. He dragged Nick along to a restaurant, visited him here a couple of times, and then he invited him on a trip to Paris. To our surprise, Nick said yes."

Molly: "They were supposed to be gone for the weekend, but Nick stayed in France for a whole month."

Rodney: "He was staying on a barge on the Seine with a family he had met. He came home and told us that he intended to settle down in Paris. He was going to try to find a job, and also mentioned that he had been in touch with Françoise Hardy. He handled all the practicalities of the trip himself, which was already unusual, and then he left, happier than we had seen him in a long time. We felt that a terrific weight had been taken off our shoulders. But something went wrong in Paris. It didn't work out. Nick came back at the end of October. It was in the following days that he started saying that if the depression continued he was afraid that he might do something stupid."

He changes his mind and again begins to write songs. This time he wants to play rock music, he confides in his parents.

Having released three albums with predominantly acoustic instruments – records that have earned him the label of folk musician and which have not sold more than a few thousand copies each – Nick feels that the time has come to change style. He acquires an electric guitar and starts composing. The big house starts to resound with feedback and thunderous riffs, as if The Who themselves were in there warming up. And just like Pete Townshend, Nick ends up smashing his instrument, with the one crucial difference that this excellent, perfectly tuned, guitar is never replaced.

"I've never seen anything like it," Rodney says. "Normally, Nick was very peaceful, bordering on the phlegmatic, but suddenly he exploded in an insane fit of rage. He shouted very loudly. We still have that guitar, well, the remains of it."

One night he comes into the kitchen where Molly is sitting with Naw the housekeeper.

"I fancy starting to play the violin," he says. "I'll go down to London tomorrow and buy one."

Molly is instantly up for it.

"Great, Nick, you can borrow my car."

Next morning when she hands him the car keys, he stares at her in confusion.

"Violin?"

He has no idea what she is talking about.

♪♪♪

Why leave me hanging on a star
When you deem me so high?

He is stranded on his own planet, far from human beings. They wouldn't listen to him when he came to them with his songs; now he himself has become deaf.

He has disappeared into a reality behind reality.

The last five songs tell of a man beyond reach.

They sound like five entries in a medical journal.

The starting point for Nick's songwriting had always been melancholia. Through the music he was able to work on his inner chaos, his anxieties and his lost loves. He recreated a harmonic world. With his guitar he called forth landscapes from a lost age and seduced his listeners into a universe of beauty. He healed the separation from his mother and father; from an unconditional love he had lost during the process of maturing from a child into an adult. He made the loss of childhood innocence a theme in his songs, and released his sorrow in tones and words.

A black-eyed dog appeared by his door.

A black-eyed dog kept staring at him.

It demanded more and more of his soul.

The last songs tell the story. The healing has stopped. His relationship with his material is gone; the magic has disappeared like the dreams of youth under a clear, blue sky.

Nick has reached a turning point.

His voice tells us; it has lost its strength. In three years it has been reduced to a plaintive sound. Now he longs to become stones and sea.

Voice from the mountain
And a voice from the sea
Voice in my neighbourhood
And a voice calling me.

At noon on Sunday 25 November, Molly found her son dead. He was lying on his bed in an awkward position, as if he had fallen forward; the only thing he was wearing was a pair of briefs. On the nightstand was a bottle of Tryptizol, anti-depressants prescribed by St. Thomas' Hospital. The bottle was empty.

"We always locked all sorts of pills away very carefully," Molly says. "With the exception of his anti-depressants. We thought they were harmless. Later on we were told that Tryptizol can be extremely dangerous for the heart.

And you must remember that Nick was physically very, very weak. Several years of severe depression had wasted away his health. It didn't take a lot to push him over the edge."

He did not leave a farewell note.

On the old mahogany desk was a folder with his early lyrics, written in black ink with a fountain pen on A4 paper. Each page was filled in his impeccable hand, full of flourishes, leaning a little towards the right, as if looking to reach the edge. He had arrived at "Fruit Tree" and the lines:

They'll all know
That you were here when you're gone.

Next to the folder was a letter to Sophia Ryde, his friend, whom he had begun seeing again after a long hiatus.

"His mood had been very up and down after he came back from France," Rodney explains. "He suffered from insomnia. He would usually get up in the middle of the night and go downstairs. Molly would always wake up when he was moving about in the music room and then she would also get up, and they would sit for hours in the kitchen and talk – if Nick felt like talking. But *that* night she did not hear him."

"I slept heavily," Molly says. "It was a real November night, cold and windy."

On the kitchen table were the mushy, yellowish, remains of a bowl of corn flakes. And in the music room one of Bach's *Brandenburg Concertos* was stuck in the inner groove on the gramophone.

"I don't really think Nick seriously meant to take his

own life," Molly adds. "But he was having a bad night. Perhaps he swallowed the pills on a sudden whim, just to get some peace. That is what he was like those last months of his life, impatient, impulsive. He would probably have regretted it in the morning."

⁂

Many of Nick's friends showed up for the funeral service in the old village church in Tanworth-in-Arden. His travel mate Richard from the Africa trip was there, as were university friends and colleagues, people from the record company and the music circles in London, women he had loved in his own quiet fashion, his collaborators Robert Kirby and John Wood; now they were all seated in church to say goodbye to the 26-year-old songwriter. What they all had in common was that they had seen less and less of him over the last three years. They listened to the vicar's speech about the village boy, the happy and capricious Nick, well-loved by his comrades, always polite and correct with adults, and they heard of the time when his house was a gathering point for all the kids in Tanworth.

After the service family and friends gathered at Far Leys.

"It was a strange experience to meet all these people," Rodney recalls. "We had no idea that Nick had such a large circle of acquaintances. Some of his friends we had met before, of course, and others he had told us about, but most of them we didn't know, and we were surprised to find that they didn't know each other either."

"A few years after Nick's death the church organ broke down and we decided to donate some of his royalties for the repairs. A new stop, the Sesquialtera, was put into the fine old organ, and the parish committee put up a small bronze plaque: 'In memory of Nicholas Drake and his music.' One day the organist came to our house and asked if he could hear a couple of Nick's songs. We played *Bryter Layter* for him, and he was tremendously taken with it. He picked out 'Sunday' and arranged the piece for organ."

Molly: "Now it's a regular part of his repertoire. He plays the piece every year around Nick's birthday. Recently he said to me: 'I play all sorts of music in this church, but after I play "Sunday" people always come up to me and ask who the composer is. Nick Drake, I say. Really? people say. We've never heard anything like it before. It's fantastic.'"

3

Nick used to pride himself. "Mum," he said to me once,
"I never get angry!" And that was true, I think.
But towards the end of his life so many things upset him.
On occasions it happened, yes, he did get angry.

MOLLY DRAKE

Existential Depression

When I visited Rodney and Molly in November of 1979 they told me that they had given Nick's guitar to one of his old friends from Cambridge. Nick's parents felt gratitude towards this man who had kept up his connection with their son right up till the end and was not scared away by his depression. After Nick's death this friend would occasionally go to Far Leys and stay there for a couple of days. "He is a doctor," Rodney explained to me. "He knows a lot about mental illness, in fact he was the one who told us about the dangers of Tryptizol – but by then it was too late, unfortunately. He knew Nick better than anyone. I wish you could meet him."

For various reasons I did not manage to get in touch with this friend of Nick's. One afternoon in April, 29 years later, I found myself travelling by Tube through London to meet him. Better late than never.

His name is Brian Wells. Today he is a psychiatrist specialising in alcohol and drug rehabilitation. His practice is in Marylebone, a part of town with many fine Georgian buildings, in Devonshire Street, to be precise. The house is a stone's throw from Regent's Park and as I cross Park Square I think of how often Nick walked here. Witchseason had their offices in Charlotte Street. I see his tall, stooping, figure before my inner eye as he disappears into the gardens one night in October, where neon signs are flashing on the walls and the lights come on in London's windows. Nick would have walked on with his long strides into the darkness. He would not have had the fare for the bus, and he would have been too weary to face the crowds on the city streets. It's a 45-minute walk from Marylebone to Haverstock Hill, and Regent's Park is actually a beautiful shortcut.

I ring the bell at one of the stately, two-storey houses in Devonshire Street.

A secretary lets me into the doctor's consulting room.

The high-ceilinged room feels intimate. Heavy curtains drape the windows facing the street and dampen the daylight and the traffic noise; the chairs are brown leather and very comfortable. There is a box of Kleenex on the table in front of me. People who come here cry. They come here to find a way through the labyrinths of the mind.

A troubled cure for a troubled mind…

The door opens and in steps Dr. Wells wearing jeans and a dark blue blazer. He is in his late fifties, keeps well, wears his shirt open; the expression on his face is relaxed and jovial. He settles down into the comfortable chair across the room and looks inquisitively at me.

"Oh, right, you'd like to see Nick's guitar?"

"Yes, please," I reply

The doctor disappears out the door with a smile on his face and returns with a steel-stringed guitar which, at first sight, seems oddly small; certainly one size smaller than my own western guitar, a cheap Japanese model.

"It's a 1972 Martin," Wells informs me.

I gently strike a chord. The guitar is perfectly in tune; Nick Drake could hardly have done better. The sound is clear and crisp, albeit not very loud; bass and treble have a nice harmony together. There are signs of wear around the hole in the dark yellow soundboard, but the fret board looks as if it has never been used. I hand the instrument back to Brian and he begins to play "From the Morning" with his eyes closed, powerfully, energetically, his fingers glide over the strings, every note rings out into the room very much as they do on Nick's record. He stops before the vocal part begins.

"A typical Nick Drake composition – you can play the riff a hundred times and still find something to explore," Brian Wells gesticulates with his right hand as he speaks. "Nick showed me the tuning and the chord shapes once when I visited him at Far Leys. That was after he had released *Pink Moon*. We were sitting in the music room listening to some of his old demo tapes. He gave me a demo of 'Fly' – actually my favourite Nick Drake song. On that tape the song has three different endings."

"I got to know Nick Drake in the summer of 1967," Wells continues soberly. "I had been a year in America where my father was stationed as a Royal Air Force pilot, and when I came to Cambridge to read medicine I started looking around for a Society I could join. In the US I had started smoking dope, so I didn't really see myself joining The Rowing Club, or just some sports club. But these guys in The Buddhist Society seemed interesting. They had long hair and looked quite cool. So I joined The Buddhist Society and that's how I ran into Nick.

The doctor stares into space a second, lost in thought.

Then he strikes a C-major chord.

"Donovan!" he exclaims. "I still think Donovan stays the distance. Listen to the early Donovan records and there you have the sixties in a nutshell. There was one album in particular that Nick and I would groove to in Cambridge – *Sunshine Superman*. We would never tire of songs like

'Hampstead Incident', 'Celeste', and 'Season of the Witch'."

"I had dragged a whole lot of records with me back from America, and I introduced Nick to Sam & Dave and other soul singers. Later on, the roles became reversed. Nick introduced me to The Byrds and Van Morrison and, significantly for me, Randy Newman. 'I Think it's Gonna Rain Today' was a song we listened to a lot."

"Nick was like an elder brother in some ways. We were always a little bit superior to our college mates. We distanced ourselves from the guys with short hair; we didn't hang out with the ambitious types. We were long-haired, cool people smoking dope."

"The Nick I met via a fellow from The Buddhist Society looked exactly like the guy on the cover of *Five Leaves Left*. Same jacket, same shirt, same air of reflective cool. He was friendly, but also aware of his image as a bit of a mysterious outsider. He kept his various groups of friends separate from one another. I was one of his Cambridge friends. I was never introduced to Joe Boyd and that whole hip music crowd he was involved with in London."

"In Cambridge I knew him as happy, enthusiastic, and really engaged in his music. We drank, smoked pot, and usually had a good and amusing time. But things changed. After he moved to London he began to withdraw more and more into himself."

Was that related to drug use?

"As far as I can tell – No. Nick definitely smoked marijuana, that is true, but he was very far from being the type who ran around stoned all day. I remember when he used to live on Haverstock Hill; that was during the months of *Bryter Layter*. I would sometimes come around with a joint, but Nick would push it away. He had stopped smoking.

He would sit there quietly. I didn't know what was going on in his head – I felt awkward and would usually leave after a while."

"There is one thing I would like to say. Drug use was not the main cause of his emotional condition. Nick might have tried heroin with someone like John Martyn, I don't know, but he never used it on a regular basis. That is a myth created by the media. Nick was not a drug addict. Nor did he have a formal mental illness like schizophrenia."

"The way I see it, he developed an existential depression. That is a form of depression which I doubt is treatable with Prozac – or with Tryptizol, which was what one prescribed back then. Nick knew very well what a great songwriter he was, but he had a fragile personality. He felt that the people for whom he was writing these songs were not hearing them. They were not buying his records. Audiences would sit and talk among themselves while he was performing. He wanted success, but was unable to fight for recognition. At some point he turned his disappointments inward. He began to feel that he had failed as a human being. An existential depression tells you that no matter what you do, life is a waste of time. Nothing is of any value. Meaningless. On top of that it was humiliating for Nick to move back to his parents' house, I mean to have to live with Mum and Dad at the age of 24. He had made three extraordinary records. You have to understand his enormous disappointment."

Brian Wells looks at the guitar on the table between us.

"The last time I visited him at Far Leys was a weekend in the summer of 1974. He had been in a bad way for quite some time, and I was prepared for him to sit in a chair and stare into space, exactly as he usually did. At some point I started to play a twelve-bar blues, and I don't know what happened to Nick, but suddenly he grabbed his saxophone and joined in the melody, and we started to improvise and make all sorts of crazy riffs. We were fooling around and laughing like in the old days, and in the middle of this magical moment Rodney and Molly came in and could hardly believe their eyes."

That one Saturday afternoon, Nick returned to the person he used to be.

For a couple of hours he was a guest star in his old self.

By early evening, after I've said goodbye to Dr. Wells, and started walking through London in the dusk, I recall a story Rodney and Molly once told me. The last night they saw their son alive, Nick had asked Molly to lend him her Linguaphone French course. He had been talking about how he missed Paris and that he would like to get back there as soon as possible. He went to bed early after slaving over French verbs in the music room. "What strikes me about our last conversation," Molly explained, "was the completely everyday quality of it. The very fact that Nick wanted to talk I saw as a sign that he was getting better. A small step in the right direction."

Time of No Reply

A few months after Nick's death, Rodney and Molly received a letter from Françoise Hardy. The French singer wanted to know exactly where and when Nick was born, because she wanted to create a birth chart for him. She wrote that she would be in touch again as soon as the horoscope was finished. Molly sent her the information she wanted, along with a few lines saying that of course she and Rodney would be very curious to see the results.

But Hardy never replied.

Perhaps the singer gave up when she saw what a complex pattern the stars formed over Rangoon, the capital of Burma, on 19 June, 1948, at a quarter past seven in the morning. A June birth puts Nick in one of the four air signs of the Zodiac: Gemini. According to astrology, people born under that sign are ambiguous, contradictory, and inscrutable. A male Gemini often finds it easy to form love relations, but due to his dual character he quickly begins to feel dissatisfied with relationships and starts telling himself that a greater, better, love is waiting on the other side of the hill. The classic Gemini is a complex character: he is a dreamer, and the fleeting nature of early summer is encapsulated in his mind.

Without drawing on any esoteric knowledge of celestial bodies and cosmic forces, we can say one thing for sure: Nick was strangely unsuited for the age. He did not fit into the generation he was born into, the cohorts that came of age in '68 with their political messages and collective project of liberation. Perhaps he would have stood out more starkly in the consumer society of the 21st century; our time, which screams out from the bottom of a rubbish heap of indifferent music and literature – for original, truthful, art.

Nick's peers were not ready to relate to a universe of moons and oceans, a quiet room in the midst of the roar of the electric Supernova, the unbearable loneliness of the heart exposed in the middle of the golden epoch of youth. Nick played chamber music at the heart of the youth revolution. He was a hippie from another century. Recognition and fame came to him in a strange backward fashion, unexpectedly, and so surprisingly that one might almost think that Jorge Luis Borges, the master of the absurd tale, had written the script.

One of the first signs that something was brewing came in 1986 when Joe Boyd released an LP with previously unknown Nick Drake recordings – *Time of No Reply* – on his Hannibal Records label. Boyd had been on an expedition into the archives of Island Records together with the American soundman Frank Kornelussen and had found eight outtakes from *Five Leaves Left*. Nick recorded the original tracks at the Sound Techniques Studio in October, November, and December of 1968. The songs came out of an unusual surplus store; they revealed an artist who consistently discarded any material that did not fit into the exact atmosphere he wanted for his debut album – regardless of the evident quality of this material.

New listeners could safely begin here. In fact, this album of discarded material pointed to three masterpieces.

Whoever encounters Nick Drake for the first time in *Time of No Reply* is not just listening to a series of demos from a dead songwriter; he or she is witnessing a narrative of the fate of a human being. The stories told insert themselves between the death of the singer and the *now* that belongs to the listener – with the magic force that time possesses. An acoustic guitar, a voice simple and pure, and a handful of lyrics that the singer has been commissioned to write.

And while time does send your questions back to you with no reply, time also has a marvellous ritual. It passes. And as it rushes along with its often imperceptible steps, people change habits and tastes, fashions shift, stars fade; so many names, so much music of one kind or another, is pushed into oblivion. But these songs that a 21-year-old poet and guitarist threw away because he found them a touch too immature and imprecise; time weighed and measured these, hid them in a treasure trove.

Nick played "Time of No Reply" and "Magic" to Robert Kirby that night in February 1968, when he appeared at Gonville and Caius with his guitar. Kirby arranged both songs for chamber ensemble, and the two friends always had them in their repertoire when they gave concerts at the various Cambridge colleges.

As for "Mayfair", this ballad about the upper-class neighbourhood in London had already been recorded by Millie Small, the Jamaican child star. Millie, who had played havoc with the world's hit lists in the mid-sixties with *My Boy Lollipop*, was aiming for a comeback in 1970.[7]

---

7   On her album *Time Will Tell*. The numbers were arranged by Robert Kirby, and it was he who persuaded Millie to record "Mayfair". In Nick Drake's lifetime three other cover versions of his songs appeared: Alexis Korner recorded "Saturday Sun" (1971), Andrew John made his own version of "Time Has Told Me" (1972), and Irish

She did a reggae version of "Mayfair". Nick himself bumbled through the song in an up-tempo jazz-style, forgot the words in the middle of the last verse, and continued to play his odd chords, laughing and mumbling.

When I was working on my biography, Nick's parents had sent me a folder containing photocopies of the lyrics that were found in Nick's room at his death, including his early unpublished songs. I knew most of them from the cassette tape that Rodney had given me on my first visit to Far Leys, but as for "Mickey's Tune", "Joey in Mind", "Outside", and "Blue Season" – I had no clue. I asked Rodney where they came from. "We have no idea," he replied. "These lyrics have always been a mystery to us. Indeed we have no actual evidence of there having been any music, although Molly and I feel sure that he must have composed some, because it was not his practice to write lyrics without music."

In 1987, about six months after the biography had been published, I started getting letters from Nick Drake fans. They wanted to know if there were recordings of the unknown lyrics that were printed at the back of the book. I replied that I had a tape with Nick Drake's recordings made at his home. If people wanted to hear the songs they would have to come see me; I did not have the means to copy the tape, nor did I want to.

---

folk band Tir Na Nog recorded "Free Ride" (1973). Of the songs about and for Nick it is worth mentioning his friend John Martyn's "Solid Air" (1972):

You've been getting too deep
You've been living on solid air
You've been missing your sleep
And you've been moving through solid air.

Despite the fact that my book had only appeared in Danish, letters kept streaming in from all corners of the globe. People from Canada, Holland, The Faroe Isles, and Norway dropped by; the rumour of the unknown songs spread like wildfire through the apparently steadily increasing number of fans. I invited complete strangers into my living room and played them the tape in the small hours of the night; the interest usually focused on those songs that were *not* on the tape. If only people could hear those last five or six songs…

When Nick was alive the world was deaf to his music.

Thirteen years after he disappeared from this world, suddenly there were people willing to travel far and wide to listen to a cassette tape of some original amateur recordings of Nick Drake with lousy sound quality.

Much later came the films, the biographies, the radio programmes, the articles in the major music magazines, and the cover songs recorded by the famous artists of the day. Nick was entered into the society for young, dead, rock icons by the critics. But unlike Jimi Hendrix, Sandy Denny, and Kurt Cobain – quite the contrary of Janis Joplin, Ian Curtis, and Jeff Buckley – Nick died a complete unknown to his contemporaries. He did not instantly become part of a generation's understanding of itself as Jim Morrison had, because he was never part of the story while alive.

All attempts to create allegories involving Nick Drake and his contemporaries, as well as later artists, and their destinies seem wrong; they reduce the story, veil it. Nick went his own way and took his own detours, for his own reasons. He followed his own winding paths, far from the broad streets of time. He died lonely. He must rest in his own unique destiny. Under the stars and planets.

Family Tree

Rodney and Molly sent me *Time of No Reply* along with a letter where they told me of the sudden interest in Nick's music they had begun to notice. They expressed a touching sense of gratitude for my biography and wrote that they could hardly wait for it to be translated. They had had visits from young Nick Drake fans, including an American who also wanted to write a biography of Nick. They had even been called up on the phone by people doing research for various articles about Nick's life and times. What came of all these projects I don't know.

"Come and see us in the merry month of May," Molly wrote me, "then we will be able to have tea in the garden."

That was in the winter of 1987. This letter turned out to be the last I would ever receive from Far Leys. Much later I discovered the reason for that. Rodney had died. From our correspondence I knew that the ageing, but physically still very active, man had heart trouble; he had undergone surgery several times over the preceding years, which had meant postponing my third trip to Tanworth.

He left behind a little black book: *For Molly*. Written in his tidy little hand, the book had a number of small chapters: *How to pay the bills. How to deal with the tax. How to set the aerials...* Through their long marriage Rodney had learned that it was no use trying to burden Molly with practicalities; she wrote poetry and songs, was a good mother and a loving wife, and that was more than enough for him. A long time ago he had bought her Far Leys because she loved the place. He had saved enough for her to remain in the house after his death, and for her to keep up a normal standard of living. It is said that Molly kept the black book with her wherever she went. She actually managed once more to cope with her grief, much as she had done when she lost her son. She took care of Far Leys for another year, and then moved to a smaller house in Tanworth-in-Arden. Molly Drake died in 1993.

Rodney, the engineer, made sure that his family stayed safe and comfortable even after he himself had gone. On the surface he seemed rather reserved and awkward, a bit of a stereotypical, conservative, English patriarch. But one did not have to spend much time with him before he let his guard down and revealed his loving, gentle nature. What struck me about Rodney was how expansive he was. One always got an urge to discuss things with him, to egg him on and provoke him, because he showed you so much respect. In Rodney's universe, poets were at the top of the social ladder, on a par with kings and war heroes. This esteem for artists was probably old-fashioned. I confess I enjoyed his company very much.

When Nick was struck by his first episode of severe depression, Rodney persuaded his son to be admitted to the St. Thomas' Hospital. Later he paid for consultations with one of England's leading experts in depressive conditions, a Harley Street psychiatrist. When that didn't work, Rodney went the anti-psychiatry route. Together with Brian Wells he joined the Philadelphia Association and participated as a family member in this programme of treatment, created by R.D. Laing. But Nick never showed up for any meetings. Still, Rodney kept looking for a cure for his boy. He wrote letters to Nick's friends, he made covert phone calls to Robert Kirby, John Martyn, and Brian Wells; did whatever he could to learn more about Nick's ways and byways.

"There was only one thing that mattered when Nick became sick," Molly explained to me in 1979. "How could I reach him? Nothing else was important. For eight months I did not leave the house. I felt that I could not leave him. I don't know if it made any difference, but I had a feeling that he clung on to us as his only hope, that he trusted that we could help him. If your son breaks an arm or a leg, you know exactly what to do. But what does one do with an injury that is invisible to the naked eye, a disease that cannot be treated with any drug? No matter what you do, you always end up choosing the wrong solution."

In a letter to her brother entitled "Dear Nick", written after his death, Gabrielle Drake writes: "Perhaps this was our parents' dilemma: they created children sure enough of themselves to want and need to fly the nest in the true sense of the word (many of our friends continued to replicate their parents' lives, but we couldn't do that), yet inadvertently, they created a bond of love so strong, it was impossible not to feel guilty about breaking away from it. Impossible not to see the value of all they had created; impossible, however much both sides wanted it, for them to follow us into the new way of thinking that was all around us at the time."

⁂

Copenhagen, October 2007. As I am re-reading *Pink Moon* and thinking back about the 25-year-old fellow who carried my name and bought a record for a pittance in a second-hand store which he found so interesting that he chose to write a biography of its creator, just as I am listening to my old Nick Drake records and the tape that Rodney gave me, an album entitled *Family Tree* appears.

Gabrielle Drake and John Wood have dug a number of amateur recordings from Aix-en-Provence and Far Leys out of the archives; Wood has cleaned the songs of the background noise and hiss, Nick's own sketches mixed in with blues classics, folk songs, and sing-along numbers that were heard in bars and on street corners throughout Europe in 1967 and '68. Thus *Family Tree* functions at once as a document of the times and a sort of probe into the workshop of a young poet and songwriter. He was inspired by guitarists such as Davy Graham, Bert Jansch, and Jackson C. Frank, but all that he gets his hands on is retuned into his own key; he plays the melodies of his mentors in his own rhythm. The deep sources of inspiration remain hidden; the trail begins and ends at Far Leys.

Maybe the key to Nick's treasure chest of songs is found somewhere in Molly's piano pieces and in the lullabies she composed for the children when they were little, maybe in the music room where the seventeen-year-old owner of a Western guitar made an appointment with Johann Sebastian Bach and black blues music. There the master of form met a great grief coming out of the Mississippi delta; two madly different styles were brought together in the small hours of dawn in improvisations that included William Blake and Charles Baudelaire.

Personally, I end where I began: with the record that I still perceive as one of the metaphysical high points to come out of the musical Supernova of the '68 generation.

The hypersensitivity of youth, the great loneliness of youth. Nick Drake hit a soft spot in me, touched the strings of a vulnerable mind.

The loneliness has not eased with age; it's just a different feeling, another nuance. Time has passed, one has survived despite it all, come to terms with existence, come to terms with death. I am sitting in the same room as when I wrote the biography, looking out of the same window. The garden, the treetops, the long lake with the pavilion at one end and the bridge at the other; the view is the same as 30 years ago. It is night. The city is asleep. Across the sky, low white October clouds drift by. The starry wheel is turning above. Between the branches of the chestnut tree there is a luminous, almost transparent, circle. I lean forward and watch it for a while. As a voice whispers from a corner of the room:

"It's a pink, pink, pink, pink, pink moon."

Discography

Five Leaves Left (Island, 1969)

Bryter Layter (Island, 1970)

Pink Moon (Island, 1972)

POSTHUMOUS RELEASES

Fruit Tree (Island, 1979)
Time of No Reply (Hannibal, 1986)
Made to Love Magic (Island, 2004)
Family Tree (Island, 2007)

COMPILATIONS

Nick Drake (Island, 1971)
Heaven in a Wild Flower (Island, 1985)
Way to Blue (Island, 1994)
A Treasury (Island, 2004)

Sources

INTERVIEWS BY GORM HENRIK RASMUSSEN

Rodney and Molly Drake, Tanworth-in-Arden:
November 1979 and August 1980

Robert Kirby, London: November 1979 and April 2008

Paul Wheeler, London: 1981 (interviewed for the
first edition of *Pink Moon* by Gillie Cunningham)

Simon Crocker, London: April 2008

Jeremy Mason, London: April 2008

Brian Wells, London: August 2008

Richard Charkin, London: August 2008

Joe Boyd: interviewed by email during 2008 and 2009

BOOKS

Baudelaire, Charles. *Les Fleurs du Mal*
(Paris: Poulet-Malassis et de Broise, 1861)

Blake, William. *The Complete Poems*,
Ed. Alicia Ostriker (London: Penguin Books, 1977)

Boyd, Joe. *White Bicycles: Making Music in the 1960s* (London: Serpent's Tail, 2006)

Camus, Albert. *Le Mythe de Sisyphe* (Paris: Librairie Gallimard, 1942)

Dann, Trevor. *Darker than the Deepest Sea: The Search for Nick Drake* (London: Portrait Publishing, 2006)

Dylan, Bob. *Chronicles: Volume One* (New York: Simon & Schuster, 2004)

Gerlach, Jes. *Depression* (Copenhagen: *PsykiatriFonden*, 2006)

Hinde, Thomas. *Paths of Progress: A History of Marlborough College* (London: James & James Publishers, 1992)

Humphries, Patrick. *Nick Drake* (London: Bloomsbury, 1997)

MacDonald, Ian. *Revolution in the Head: The Beatles' Records and the Sixties* (London: Fourth Estate, 1994)

Rasmussen, Gorm Henrik. *Pink Moon: Sangeren og guitaristen Nick Drake* (Højbjerg: Forlaget Hovedland, 1986)

Redd, Lawrence N. *Rock is Rhythm and Blues: The Impact of Mass Media* (East Lansing, Michigan: Michigan State University Press, 1974)

JOURNALS & OTHER PRINT SOURCES

Callomon, Cally von. "A Much Updated Ruin from a Much Outdated Style," *Fruit Tree*, Island Records, 2007

Creed, Jason. *Pynk Moon*, Nos. 1–17 (Surrey: 1996–99)

Drake, Gabrielle. "Dear Nick," *Family Tree*, Bryter Music, Island Records, 2007

Ferrara, Marks. "Ch'an Buddhism and the Prophetic Poems of William Blake," *Journal of Chinese Philosophy* Vol. 24 (1997)

Frederick, Robin. "Song of Aix," *Family Tree*, Bryter Music, Island Records, 2007

Freud, Sigmund. "Trauer und Melancholie," *The International Journal of Psychoanalysis* Vol. 4, No. 6 (1917), pp. 288–301

Gilbert, Jerry. "Something Else for Nick," *Sounds* (13 March 1971)

Gilbert, Jerry. "Nick Drake: Death of a Genius," *Sounds* (14 December 1974)

Hicks, Andrew. "A Memory of My Childhood Friend," *Family Tree*, Bryter Music, Island Records, 2007

Kelly, Rob. "Nick Drake," *Déja Vu* No. 3 (1977)

Lubow, Arthur. "Nick Drake," *Fruit Tree:
The Complete Recorded Works*, Island Records, 1978

MacDonald, Ian. "Exiled from
Heaven," *Mojo* (January 2000)

McKnight, Connor. "In Search of Nick
Drake," *ZigZag* No. 42 (1974)

Paphides, Peter. "Stranger to the World,"
The Observer (25 April 2004)

Sandison, David. "Nick Drake:
The Final Retreat," *ZigZag* No. 49 (1974)

Segal, Hanna. "A Psycho-Analytical Approach
to Aesthetics," *International Journal
of Psycho-Analysis*, No. 33 (1952)

OTHER MEDIA

Berkvens, Jeroen. *A Skin Too Few:
The Days of Nick Drake*, Humanist Broadcasting
Foundation, Hilversum, Netherlands, 2000

Clements, Tim. *A Stranger Among Us:
Searching for Nick Drake*, BBC2, BBC Bristol, 1999

Nick Drake: Under Review, Chrome Dreams,
New Malden, Surrey, 2007, and Sexy Intellectual, 2007
(the writer and the director wish to remain anonymous)

Note on the Author

Gorm Henrik Rasmussen (*b.* 1955) is a poet living in Copenhagen, Denmark. He has published novels, short stories, poems, and works of non-fiction. His subjects include eccentrics and strange places of the northern part of Jutland, where he was born and raised. He has received several literary awards from The Danish Arts Foundation and The Danish Arts Council.

For more music books with extra thrust visit
rocket88books.com